Trial by Fire

This Book Belongs To:

Personal Journal - Page 143

Date: _____

Donated By:

My Family and I: Cory, Crystal, Rex and Kimber.

Chaplain Grady and family: (R-L) Emily, Hannah, Joshua and Leah.

Endorsements

"Sgt. Russell served the Tennessee Highway Patrol with unwavering dignity. His service brought a positive perspective to the law enforcement community as a whole. *Trial by Fire* tells one of the most inimitable stories of our era. It's a great read!"

- Governor Bill Haslam
Tennessee State Governor

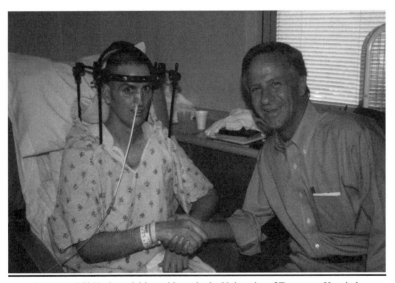

Governor Bill Haslam visiting with me in the University of Tennessee Hospital.

Endorsements

Endorsements

"This is a must read book for all first responders, military personnel and their families. It will benefit all who read it, as Trooper Sergeant Russell's life story and spiritual journey is a sermon we all need to experience and take to heart the lessons shared. His trial is the divine intervention others may need to survive whatever struggles they may be having."

- Chief David Rausch
Knoxville Police Department
Knoxville, TN

"I've just finished my second time reading through *Trial by Fire* and what a tremendous encouragement Sgt. Russell's life story has been to me. I highly recommend this book to everyone in, or associated with, law enforcement. Whether officer, supervisor, retiree, family member, chaplain or friend, I believe you will receive inspiration, enlightenment and encouragement as well."

- Mark Clements
President, International Conference of Police Chaplains
(ICPC)

Photo Credits

Front cover photo: Property of Lowell Russell

Family photos: Property of Lowell Russell and Paul Grady

Endorsement Photo: Property of Lowell Russell

Back cover photo: Courtesy Knoxville News Sentinel, used by permission

Back cover inserted photos: Property of Lowell Russell and Paul Grady

Pages: 5, 7, 9, 10, 16, 18, 19, 24, 30, 38, 43, 46, 48, 52, 54, 56, 57, 58, 61, 63, 68, 75, 84, (top 86), 102, 104, 118, 119, 120, Property of Lowell Russell and Paul Grady

Pages: 28, 77, 80, Property of Stacey Wood-Heatherly, used by permission

(Bottom) Page 86: Courtesy Knoxville News Sentinel, used by permission

Page 95: Property of Lowell Russell and WATE News, used in joint cooperation

Page: 116, Property of Allyson Mason, used by permission

Page: 117, Property of Laurie McDaniel, used by permission

Trial by Fire

The True Story of Tennessee State Trooper Sgt. Lowell Russell

By: Sgt. Lowell Russell and Dr. Paul Grady

Bookmasters Printing Company

Copyright © 2014

Lowell Russell and Paul Grady

PO Box 777
Vonore, TN 37885

Disclaimer

The opinions expressed in this book are solely those of the authors and do not necessarily reflect the views of the individuals who are quoted, those who have given their endorsement or those of the publishing company.

While the authors have made every effort to provide accurate internet addresses at the time of publication, neither the publisher nor the authors assumes any responsibility for errors or for changes that occur after publication.

All quoted material is cited exactly (including grammar, punctuation and misspellings) as it appears in printed sources. Within the quoted matter, including Bible verses, italicized material is emphasized by the source; bold print indicates emphasis by the author of this book. All Scripture used is as derived from the King James Version of the Bible.

ISBN No. 978-1-60208-349-3
Library of Congress Control Number: TBD
First Printing, November, 2014

For printer information:
Bookmasters
30 Amberwood Parkway
Ashland, OH 44805
estimating@bookmasters.com
(800) 537-6727
http://www.bookmasters.com

Dedication

This book is dedicated to two wonderful groups of people. First, are our brothers and sisters of the thin blue line. Thank you for your daily sacrifice. Stay safe out there. Watch your six, your partner's six and keep that head on a swivel!

Second, this book is dedicated to all the men and women of our great military. We extend to you the same thank you for all that you do to keep our country safe and free from all enemies, both foreign and domestic. We pray daily for your safety. Thank you, thank you, THANK YOU!

Acknowledgements

It would be extremely difficult to begin to list all the names of those who had a hand in this book coming to fruition. If we were to try there would no doubt be someone unintentionally left out. We will, however, say a specific thanks to Linda Holt-Milam, Linda Grady, Emily Grady, Emily McQuate and Jerry Traxler. You were a great editing, proofreading and design team. Thank you!

Table of Contents

Foreword

When a minister's phone rings in the wee hours of the morning, someone is usually in trouble. I was in Nashville, Tennessee, on March 13, 2012, attending a meeting. The jangling of the phone roused me to consciousness. The call was to tell me that my friend, Tennessee State Trooper Sgt. Lowell Russell, had been involved in a fiery crash on Interstate 40 in Knoxville, Tennessee. The graphic video I later watched showed a giant ball of fire, and a mass of twisted and charred metal that had been Lowell's car. I thought to myself, "No one could go through that and live to tell the story." Miraculously, Lowell Russell *did* live through that crash, and this book is *his* story. In fact, this book is full of inspirational stories from Lowell's life.

I have always loved great storytelling. When I hear stories, I hear God's voice reminding me where I have been, telling me where I am now, and pointing me in the direction I need to go. Lowell's stories do that and much more. They serve to remind us that life is made up of moments. We tend to see lives in terms of "big" and "key" events, but these rich stories remind us that all the moments of our lives are big in the eyes of the Lord. Wherever we are in life, we can hear Him say something special to us if we will simply listen.

In closing, some might say stories are a waste of time, and that it is dangerous to live in the past. However, when something of value falls out of your vehicle, it is wise to stop, turn around, and pick it up before you journey on. Tragically, our hurry-up age has lost some precious values from our past, and refuses to reverse direction to reclaim them. Values such as family, forgiveness, and faith are often lost. Lowell Russell's experiences made him stop and rethink life. His book can help us do the same.

- Dr. Lon Shoopman
Senior Pastor
First Baptist Church
Madisonville, TN

Introduction

I would like to start off by thanking you for taking time out of your busy schedule to read this book. I am humbled that you would take an interest in my story. While, yes, this is my story, it's about much more than who I am. There isn't anything special about me, but rather that God chose to use me in a very unusual fashion, to be a help and encouragement to others. Essentially, my whole life I desired to be a public servant. I was able to fulfill that role for nearly twenty years as a deputy sheriff and a highway patrolman.

After my wreck there were many uncertainties. One thing was for sure: I wanted to continue in public service someway, somehow. While the opportunity to climb into a cruiser may have passed, the desire within me to serve was stronger than ever. I became involved in many military veteran functions, and founded the LCpl Frankie Watson Memorial Scholarship Fund (see appendix). As busy as I was, something still felt like it was missing.

That's when it happened – the answer to this void came at an unexpected time. I was attending a Thanksgiving dinner at my local THP branch. As I was preparing to leave Chaplain Grady approached me and asked if we could walk together to my truck. As we walked, he shared with me his vision for this book. This was it! The burden to share my story on a larger scale could be accomplished through this venue. This is what was missing!

Chaplain Grady and I have a very unique relationship. The first time we met was when Frankie

Watson was killed in combat (See Chapter 6). While we chatted via the phone and texted several times over the next few months, I didn't see him again until we worked together on a fiery car crash that resulted in a fatality. Although we kept in contact, it wasn't until I was involved in my own fiery crash that we saw each other once again. The first words I remember Chaplain Grady saying to me in the hospital went something like this: "Lowell, every time I see you someone is either dying or in a fiery car crash; we need to stop meeting like this!" I am happy to report those scenarios seem to have abated.

My hope and prayer for you, the reader, is that this book serves to strengthen you to continue on in the face of adversity. If you are going through your own trial of sorts, know that there is a true blessing waiting on the other side if you will endure. As hard as it may seem at times, life does go on, even when your personal apple cart has been upset. Blessings to you!

-     Sgt. Lowell Russell

Real, true, abiding friends are hard to find these days. My partner in this project, Lowell Russell, is just that – a true friend. Although our friendship was born in adversity, it was one that was forged in a special love that the brotherhood of the thin blue line can only afford. As he has previously attested, every time Lowell and I met professionally we were involved in the darker side of the job. This only served to strengthen the bond of our relationship.

From day one the thing that stuck out to me about Sgt. Russell is his servant's heart. Having grown up in the home of a minister and having been involved in both ministry and law enforcement, I have been afforded the opportunity to be around some very special public servants. Lowell ranks high in that category. As you will read in this book, he has sacrificed his time, talents, and personal resources to go above and beyond the call of duty to help others. This is a rare attribute in today's society.

In Matthew 25:31-40, Jesus Christ, while teaching his disciples, gives us an example of what a true servant is. He says in vs. 37-40: *"Then shall the righteous answer him, saying, Lord, when saw we thee an hungred, and fed thee? or thirsty, and gave thee drink? When saw we thee a stranger, and took thee in? or naked, and clothed thee? Or when saw we thee sick, or in prison, and came unto thee? And the King shall answer and say unto them, Verily I say unto you,* **Inasmuch as ye have done it unto one of the least of these my brethren, ye have done it unto me.**" This is a great definition of the character of the man of whom you are about to read.

A unique perspective to the life changing events that happened to Lowell can be found by comparing Scripture with Scripture. While the devil may have thought he garnered a victory by this tragic event, what has followed in Sgt. Russell's life shows that Zechariah 3:2 rings true: *"...O Satan; even the LORD that hath chosen Jerusalem rebuke thee:* **is not this a brand plucked out of the fire?** " The spirit that Lowell expressed through this event rang with similarity to that of Job in Job 13:15: *"Though* **he slay me,** *yet will* ***I trust in him."*** Lowell was able to keep this mentality because he knew the same truth that Joseph knew when he was sold into slavery by his own brothers. Genesis 50:20 says, *"But as for you, ye thought evil against me; but* ***God meant it unto good."***

There are two major themes that are interwoven throughout this book. One is that every trial you face in life is there to prepare you for the next. There is an old saying that goes something like this: "Did it ever occur to you that nothing occurs to God?" Nothing happens to you by accident. There is a divine will and plan in everything we endure this side of eternity. God is preparing you for the next events to come in life. Romans 5:3-4 says, *"...knowing that* ***tribulation*** *worketh* ***patience;*** *And patience,* ***experience;*** *and experience,* ***hope."***

The second theme is that you have the ability to make of life what you will. You can be dictated to by your circumstances, or you can dictate to your circumstances. We were taught in academy: "What doesn't kill you makes you stronger." This mentality is not only what kept Sgt. Russell alive, but also what made him thrive in his new life.

Much of what is written in the latter half of this book came out of a special spiritual journey Lowell and I took together. Many dinners, phone calls, and in home visits produced what you will read in the following pages. If you are a law enforcement officer going through your own critical incident or personal struggles, or if you are from any other walk of life, may this book serve as a source of rich encouragement to you as you endure that fiery trial. Know that you can come out the other side a stronger and purer "you" than when you went in.

-     Dr. Paul Grady

Chapter 1
THOSE WERE THE DAYS
"Let no man despise thy youth..."
I Timothy 4:12

Someone once said that law enforcement officers (LEOs) were born with the job in their DNA. I'm not much of a scientist, so I don't know if that is exactly true, but hey, I'll take the bait. After nearly twenty years in law enforcement I can tell you this much: it isn't just a job – it's a destiny. Like being a minister, it's a calling. I believe if you take a look at my life you can see the evidence that substantiates this claim. I didn't come from a proud, long line of law enforcement officers as many have. Knowing me from a child, I'd have been the last person you'd have thought would wear the badge. There's no doubt in my mind – it's definitely a calling – not a selection. Allow me, if you will, to paint the picture for you.

It was August 25, 1975, at 2045 hours was when this little fella came screaming into the world. I'm sure my lungs sounded like a siren, but there was no emergency attached. It was just a bouncing little baby boy that wanted the world to know that he had arrived on scene and was ready to take on the world. Larry Lowell Russell was here (duty belt not included)!

During my childhood I would have many trials to endure, but, thankfully, I was blessed with good health. In fact, when I had my accident in 2012, the doctors told me that my survival was due in part to the good physical condition I was in. My body was accustomed to being put under duress, aiding in my fight not to die, even while in a coma.

I still have a few peculiar memories from my youth. While I enjoyed my adolescence, the trials that I would withstand would come early and often. I was born to Larry and Shirley Russell of Maryville, Tennessee. We lived out "in the sticks" on Laws Chapel Road. I'm sure you've heard of the term "growing up dirt-poor," but that wasn't our case. In hindsight, it seemed at times that the dirt was wealthier than we were. I remember one time going to the road to get the mail and in it was a Social Security statement for my dad. It noted that he didn't even make $14,000 that year. That may have been fine for a burger flipping teen to live on, but it made it pretty tough for a family of four. We rarely were able to go out to eat, with the exception of special occasions which were usually fast food restaurants. This was all that we could afford.

The first home I remember living in was not one that you would brag about to your friends. It was a rundown, single-wide trailer with paper thin walls and corresponding holes in the floor. I can remember one night as a young child going to bed and waking up in pain, crying. My feet felt as if they were on fire! When Mom and Dad rushed in to inspect, they discovered that a rat had crawled into my bed and had bitten me on my toes. I recall my parents being extremely upset about it. However, we were so poor we couldn't afford to go to the emergency room. Mom treated my wounds as best as she could and Dad set traps for the rat. He sat by the hole for the rest of the night with a 20 gauge shotgun, just daring that rat to come back out for some pure redneck justice. It was the mercy of God that I didn't get an infection or lose my toes.

The first time I remember hearing my mother cry was at the age of six. Through those same paper thin walls, I heard the phone ring late one night. Someone was calling to tell us that my Papaw, Fred Shaw, had died. He was the first person I knew who died. I loved him and my Mamaw Mary very much. I was saddened that I wouldn't have the opportunity to make many memories with him. Because I was his little buddy, he gave me the nickname "Wowo," although, thankfully, it didn't stick!

I'm glad that youthful ignorance is at its peak when you are just a little runt or else I probably would have developed a complex. Every school I went to throughout my K-12 years closed down. Looking back, I probably stressed them out and when the school year was over they shouted, "No mas!" and closed the doors. While, yes, I am speaking tongue-in-cheek about the "why" the various schools closed down, I did have a lot of struggles when it came to learning. Part of that may have come from how frequently I changed schools. Being at a new school meant a new environment and new teachers, both working together to produce new struggles with my learning abilities.

When I was in the second grade I transferred to a new elementary school. While you wouldn't think that things would be much different, at the end of the school year I found myself sitting on the receiving end of a negative parent-teacher meeting. I had failed the second grade. No, that isn't a typo – second grade! My biggest struggle was with reading. Having a hard time reading caused me to lag in all other subjects. My teacher put me in a special reading class the next time around and I passed. Two times through the second grade and I could shout out the alphabet better than anyone else! Several of my brothers and sisters from various departments and agencies who knew this part of my story have "enjoyed" reminding me of it… man, sometimes you just gotta love the brotherhood!

A true regret I have is how little effort I gave to my schooling. I had struggles and I didn't work to apply myself. I remember thinking to myself on the aforementioned day when I saw my dad's Social Security statement, "Yeah, I'll never go to college." While I'm thankful that sentiment changed over time, I placed myself at a major disadvantage, allowing my circumstances to control me instead of using them to make me a better person. It was a wakeup call for me when I almost flunked again in the eighth grade. I really didn't want to do summer school or repeat a grade all over again. Up to that point I simply hadn't cared about my education.

The two troublemakers – Cory and me.

I wasn't an evil child per se, but I could be mischievous at times. Quite often my focus was more on having fun than on learning. At the end of my eighth grade year my class went on a trip to Washington D.C. They stuck four of us smelly kids together in each room. The hotel we were in had an older design that would let the windows open just wide enough to stick your hands out. We got bored waiting for breakfast on that first morning and decided it would be funny to pour water on the unsuspecting people walking along the sidewalk below us. We sure were having a blast and thought we were in the clear until we came downstairs to see the wet and very hot heads complaining. The only saving grace that morning was that they weren't able to figure out if it was us or kids from a different school group that were there at the same time.

All humor aside, despite my occasional acts of mischievousness, I was raised to be honest. This was something I believe kept me from turning into a true problem child. The school issues I had stemmed from a major lack of confidence in my ability to make good grades. I thought I couldn't do it; therefore, I didn't try. If there is any young person reading this book, I beg you NOT TO HAVE THAT ATTITUDE. No matter what, apply yourself. If the best grade you can get is D-, be proud of it. Be able to lay your head on your pillow at night knowing you put your all on the line. Never wish you did more. Everything changed for me when I started high school. We'll deal more with that in the next chapter.

As an officer I've been asked many times when I decided to become a cop. That isn't a question that is easy to answer. I can't remember any specific day or time, but I know as a little sprout I wanted to be a LEO. When I was in kindergarten my mom bought me a "growing book" called *Lowell's School Days* that had a place in which each year you could write down your height, weight, and what you wanted to be when you grew up. With the exception of three years, every year I filled it out putting down that I wanted to be a police officer. Those three exceptions were years I had decided to be an astronaut, race car driver, and a cowboy. I guess I somewhat fulfilled those three ambitions in getting my pilots' license, driving fast, and carrying a gun!

This is my actual copy of *Lowell's School Days*.

7

My first "ride along" came on a beautiful Sunday evening when I was about eight years old. We arrived early for choir practice at Piney Level Baptist Church when our choir director, Tony Taylor, offered me a ride. At the time he was a Blount County Sheriff's Deputy. Our ride along lasted all of about five minutes as we drove up Piney Level Church Road and back, but I remember feeling right at home in his cruiser. Even then I knew I wanted to be a police officer.

As a kid I hardly realized we were poor. While growing up I truly enjoyed life; it was very simple back then. I didn't have the newest gaming system, shoes, clothes, etc…; God forbid, we didn't even have cable TV! We had a whopping three stations, and yes, you guessed it: I was the guy who had the privilege of running outside to adjust the main antenna so whatever TV show we were watching would come in clearer. My brother Cory and I didn't melt our minds on TV all day long. We played outside until we were sunburned, or just completely worn out… or hungry.

As a child I was frequently drugged; drug to church every Sunday morning, Sunday night, and most Wednesdays, that is. My mother was a strong woman of faith. It didn't matter how little income we had, she always made sure there was enough gas in the tank so we could go to church. I don't recall ever seeing a Saturday evening go by when Mom wasn't at the kitchen table figuring out how much ten percent of Dad's paycheck was and writing out an offering check to the church. She was a woman of deep conviction and dedication.

Mom made sure we were in church on Sundays!

We lived next door to my loving grandparents, Fred and Mary Russell. Sunday afternoon after church was reserved for time at "Mamaw and Papaw's" house. Sunday dinner with the entire family – that's when life truly was at its best. Papaw had a little eighty acre farm that we helped him work. This is where most of our food came from. There is something special about growing and/or harvesting your own food that just makes it taste better.

Looking at pictures with Dad while camping with Papaw and the family.

Although I enjoyed working on the farm, I never was much of an outdoorsman. I wasn't a big fan of camping except for when Papaw would hook up his old-fashioned wagon. This was something exceptional and unique. We would have an old-fashioned campfire cookout that made me feel like a cowboy (with the addition of roasting marshmallows). Our night would be topped off with a square dance around the campfire. I know it may sound hokey, but when you are spending time with your family, it's the "who" not the "what" that matters. When the family was together, life was great. Truly, *Those Were the Days*.

Chapter 2
CHANGING OF THE TIMES

"O God, thou hast taught me from my youth: and hitherto have I declared thy wondrous works."

Psalms 71:17

High school – what a weird world that was! While I am glad the drama is over, it was a place marked with many positive changes in my life. I believe that the foundation for me to be able to survive (both physically and emotionally) my biggest personal trial was laid in these blossoming, yet awkward years. This time was also the marker for the saddest test I had yet to endure. It's not an uncommon ordeal young people have to face in our day and age, but I wouldn't wish it on anyone.

During the summer of my ninth grade year we moved the next county over to Vonore, Tennessee. It was there that my brother Cory and I attended Vonore High School. I learned a valuable life lesson from my teachers about how they and other mentors are the architects for how a student can be molded. As previously stated, I had great difficulty with learning while growing up, many issues stemming from a lack of confidence. While I had great teachers in my elementary and middle school years, it wasn't until high school that I had a mentor that took an interest in me, helping to turn the "learning tide." That man was Coach Dave Evans.

Being a new kid on the block doesn't help much when you are already having confidence issues. Call it a sixth sense, discernment, experience, or call it what you will, but something made Coach Evans take a particular interest in me. Out of all the students, he saw *me*. I first met coach at school orientation where he advised me that he needed a new basketball team manager. Elmer Dupes, the current manager, would be graduating that year. Coach wondered if I would be interested in training with him for the position. Would I?! Yes, I would! Little did I know how much that small commitment would permanently, positively impact my life.

The last few weeks of summer went by fast like they usually do at this age, and I found myself once again at a new school. This time I was the low man on the totem pole – a freshman! I feared I was going into another cycle of frustrations and struggles. D-R-E-A-D was all I felt. That all changed when Coach Evans walked up to me on the first day of school and asked me if I was still willing to be his assistant. To say I was blown away is an understatement. With as many students as there were at the school I assumed that he would forget about our prior conversation and I would be able to slink away and disappear into the crowd. If no one saw me I could just exist and get out of school – if I'm lucky – four years later.

When coach took an interest in me it caused a positive ripple effect in other areas of my life. For once, someone who wasn't family believed in me, making me feel like I could do more than I ever thought I could. Prior to this, I had always thought that teachers were a higher class in society and that they didn't have time for poor kids. I was in essence a second-class citizen in my own mind. I really didn't even believe that teachers cared all that much. My youthful perception was that it was just a job to them. Whether I was right or wrong up 'till then isn't the point, perception is reality. I hadn't yet had a teacher that I had connected with. When coach *personally* took me under his wing, my perspective was transformed.

With a new outlook and a little dose of encouragement my grades started slowly improving throughout the year. Finally, I was learning the value of applying one's self. Thanks to coach, I started maturing at a rapid pace. I spent the rest of the basketball season learning the team manager responsibilities from Elmer. Every morning before school he and I would fill the coke machine for coach. I went to every game, watching and learning what I would be doing as the new coach's assistant for the next three years. I thought I was just doing something fun, but little did I realize that coach was instilling in me such values as commitment, loyalty, teamwork, and friendship. The best things he imparted to me were responsibility and a strong work ethic.

Coach knew a little about our family's financial situation and would help me find odd jobs around the school so I could make an extra buck or two. I spent many nights as a janitor cleaning up after games, school dances, and many suchlike functions. During the summers I would also mow lawns to earn some money. It wasn't much, but I was learning that a good work ethic isn't about money. It's about something much bigger than that –You get one shot at life and that's it. Can you go to sleep at the end of each day with a clean and clear conscience? The way the Bible says it is: *"Whatsoever thy hand findeth to do, do it with thy might; for there is no work, nor device, nor knowledge, nor wisdom, in the grave, whither thou goest,"* (Ecclesiastes 9:10).

By my sophomore year things were starting to come together for me. My grades were continuing to improve and I was gaining more and more friends with each passing day. I was not only developing lasting relationships with my classmates but was also seeing the management in a different light. I was becoming friends with the teachers, staff, and counselors. School proved to be a night and day experience in just a year's time.

Elmer had graduated and I was now the one and only assistant. He had had a concession stand set up in the gym where he used to sell various snack items to help coach raise money for the athletic program and now it was my turn. Its popularity grew over time and by my senior year it became a pretty common hangout spot. Folks used to call my little corner "Lowell's Bar and Grill."

During the year, coach bought a home close to mine and I found myself spending a lot of time there with him and his family. This was due in part to changes occurring at my home. As much as I dearly loved my parents, they weren't getting along. I yearned for the stability of a good home environment like I found at Coach Evans' house.

15

Subject

These people
eachers. talk
ends. There
t choose not
same area
in and sweat
lass. These
d their time
tball. And.
are not eat-
nitely are
lunch.

Picture from my High School Annual of "Lowell's Bar and Grill."

As far as school goes, my junior year was pretty much more of the same. Things were going well for me. However, things weren't getting better at home. The roughest trial I faced in my youth was about to hit. It was worse than all the financial and scholastic struggles I had endured previously. The talk that I knew deep down was coming, but hoped wouldn't, had finally come: Mom and Dad were getting a divorce. It's often been said that those injured the most in a breakup are the children. I believe that to be true. Reasons for the divorce aside, I loved my parents and didn't want to see them separate. Just when life looked like it was going in the right direction, my little seventeen-year-old world was turned upside down.

Both parents had been there my whole life. Now, it was gone. I felt sick about it. No child truly wants to pick sides between their parents. My brother Cory and I were now forced to choose. Who do we live with? For some, such decisions may sound easy, but they aren't. They are especially difficult for a child who is being forced to try to think like an adult and make adult choices. Cory and I decided to stay with Dad in Vonore so we could continue at our school while Mom moved back to Maryville. We would still see her on a regular basis and be close to her, but things had changed.

I was heartbroken over a broken family. Searching for answers, I continued spending time with Coach Evans, his wife Jackie, and their son Nic. They treated me like a second son. I spent many nights there, especially while my folks were going through their divorce. No disrespect is pointed toward my parents at all; I loved them dearly to their dying days. The Evans family allowed me a grounding that I desperately needed. I'm eternally grateful to them for "adopting" me into the family. Over time, I would come to peace with this trial and learn to have love and forgiveness toward my parents. I don't think this would have been possible if coach and his family hadn't been there for me. The lesson I learned is to take every opportunity life gives you to help someone. You may be making more of an impact than you realize.

Mello Yellow helped me survive my high school years.

By the time my senior year rolled around I was pretty well adjusted to everything. Through coach I had made good inroads with my education and relationship building skills. One special relationship that budded for me was with my principal, Mr. Mike Lowry. As I matured, it was clear to me that I wanted to do one of two things: I would either become a math teacher or a law enforcement officer. My desire to work in some form of public service was due to how much I felt the staff cared about me as an individual. The clincher for me was Principal Lowry, who also served as a boating officer for the Tennessee Wildlife Resources Agency (TWRA). His future influence swayed me more towards being a LEO than a teacher. In the summer between school years he would let me come and do ride alongs on the TWRA boat to get some law enforcement exposure. It did a lot to fuel the fire that was already burning in me for the profession.

Prior to being my principal, Mr. Lowry was my history teacher. He asked me if I would be interested in being an office aid for the school. There was no way I could refuse one of my heroes! I would arrive at 0630 hours every morning to prep the office and would stay and help until 0800 hours when school started. December 24, 2013, was a sad day when Mr. Lowry passed away unexpectedly while we were writing this book. He was a great man who left the world a better place than when he entered it.

My favorite picture of Principal Lowry and Frankie Watson.

While my confidence had grown tremendously in high school, I still had the thought in my person that I wasn't good enough for college. I had grown up poor and knew I couldn't afford it. However, I had many friends that were graduating and going on to college and the thought that "maybe I could" started surfacing. I made an appointment to speak with my guidance counselor, Ms. Mary Kefauver. She felt college was within my reach and helped me fill out financial aid papers. I know this subject may seem controversial to some who read this, but I am thankful for the program. It provided the opportunity for me to go to college.

I started Roane State Community College in the fall of 1994 and continued through 1996 when I shifted my ambitions more directly towards law enforcement. I enrolled in the Cleveland State Community College Police Academy in the fall 1997 class. This also gave me twenty-one credits toward my criminal justice degree. I completed the academy but was unable to attend the graduation because in the meantime, I had been selected by the Tennessee Highway Patrol (THP) to attend their academy to become a trooper. I finally completed my college education in the fall of 2009, earning an Associate's Degree in Criminal Justice from Roane State.

In the end, I graduated seventh in my class in high school. I went on to graduate from the above mentioned college, law enforcement academies, and the Tennessee Bureau of Investigation (TBI) academy in 2008. Not bad for a fella that failed the second grade, eh? The proud male ego in me would like to take credit for it, but the truth is, without people like Coach Evans, Principal Lowry, Counselor Kefauver, and many others, there is no doubt my life would be drastically different.

A few of those "many others" I would also like to recognize for being great role models throughout my high school years are Robert Costner and Lynn Gentry. They were two faithful folks, who I found to be a regular source of encouragement. Dr. Bob Lovingood, director of Monroe County Schools, and several of my teachers (Larry Russell, Tim Blankenship, Priscilla Gregory, Mary Lowe, and Kay Rouse) were always there for the students. Officers who took a special interest in me and fanned the flames for law enforcement were: TWRA Officers Randy Huskey, and Doug McKenzie; Vonore, Tennessee Police Officer Stacy DeLoach; and Madisonville, Tennessee Police Officer Greg Smith. I am thankful to God for using these great people in such impactful ways during the *Changing of the Times*.

Chapter 3
HUMBLE BEGINNINGS
"For who hath despised the day of small things?"
Zechariah 4:10

Building on the experiences I had with Principal Lowry, I now knew what direction I was going to go with my life: I was going to be a police officer. I felt this afforded me the best opportunity at a life of public service. While I was the first in my household to enter law enforcement or to go to college, it helped to open the door for my brother, Cory, to enter the profession as well. Today he also serves as an outstanding trooper for the Tennessee Highway Patrol.

The opportunity for me to join the thin blue line brotherhood came when I was hired by the Monroe County Sheriff's Office on Friday, May 5, 1995. I was called in for an interview and all I can say is they must have been desperate for help because they hired this greenhorn as an Auxiliary Deputy Sheriff. I stayed on the force in this capacity for a little over a year until later in 1996 when I hit the "big leagues" and went to part-time status. The sheriff at the time, Doug Watson, called me into his office and told me that he needed me to function as a process server. My duties mainly consisted of serving civil papers (subpoenas, orders

22

of protection paperwork, etc.) and the occasional criminal warrant. Sheriff Watson was very pro-education and knew I was planning to go back to Roane State Community College that fall. When he assigned me the position, he told me he would work around my college schedule and guarantee 20-30 work hours a week. It's men like this that made me love the uniform. I'm very thankful for Sheriff Watson and the start he gave me in law enforcement. Without him I wouldn't be where I am today.

Needless to say, "wet behind the ears" didn't begin to describe me in those early days. I was very young and lacked any law enforcement experience when I started at the sheriff's office. I was very anxious to start working as a deputy and I remember thinking the whole process of ordering uniforms and equipment, and completing my physical and psychological evaluations was taking forever. I was so eager to go to work that when it all finally came together and my uniforms arrived, I opened up the shirt and put it on straight out of the box. I'm sure those of you in law enforcement can remember those feelings. Time seemed to stand still – that was nearly twenty years ago now. Time flies when you're having fun!

Being nineteen years old, I thought I was ready to take on the world. On my first day, when I suited up I didn't put much thought or preparation into my appearance as I pinned on my brass and went to work. That's when I learned my first important lesson on appearance with Captain Joe Grant. I earned a much-needed chewing out as he went on to explain to me how important it is for an officer to look his best on the job and the power of officer presence; our first line of defense.

Early days at Monroe County Sheriff's Office.

By the second week on the job, I had this whole law enforcement thing figured out, and NOW was well on my way to conquering the world (or so I thought). I had my uniform ironed and squared away. My brass was nice and polished, and this time, properly pinned on. When I reported for duty, I walked into the jail, and my supervisor told me he needed me to take an inmate to a doctor's appointment. I was given the keys to a sleek 1991 Ford Crown Victoria, which was parked across the street, and I was ready to go. Wow! I had a uniform, gun, badge, and now a car! I had survived my first week on the job, and the chewing by the captain. I was officially a veteran officer.

I walked over to start the cruiser and noticed (my detective skills kicking in) there was frost on the windshield. Using all the wisdom and law enforcement experience I had gained, I scraped off just enough frost to be able to see out a small hole. I was going to drive around back and get the prisoner ready for transport while the car warmed up and allow the rest of the frost to melt. As I was pulling out of the parking lot I attempted to make a hard right turn onto the street but failed see a big ditch (my detective skills *not* kicking in). I ended up driving the patrol car's right rear tire into the ditch, bottoming the cruiser onto its frame. Man, this LEO stuff is harder than it looks, and full of lessons to learn every day! It was a *long* short walk back into the jail. Before I could complete my assignment we had to get a wrecker to pull the cruiser out of the ditch. There were many similar growing pains, but my thin blue line family showed much patience, training me and helping me to mature along the way.

I truly believe there is no such thing as a self-made man. Every "individual" is in fact, a composite of the influences of many people in their lives, both the good and the bad. One such God-send for me was Mr. Bob Griffitts. Mr. Griffitts is Chief of Staff for United States Congressman John J. Duncan Jr., and a longtime family friend. He put his own integrity and reputation on the line, as a reference for me, when I applied for the Tennessee Highway Patrol. He was an integral part in my being selected for the academy. Another was a very dear lady by the name of Nancy Sue Talent, who worked for the Sheriff's office, and was instrumental in me surviving my early days there.

After several months of testing, interviewing, etc., I was offered a job with THP and a spot in Academy Class 898 in Nashville, Tennessee. I had been with the Monroe County Sheriff's Office just shy of three years when I began with THP on Sunday, March 1, 1998. While I would miss working with my Monroe County brothers and sisters, I looked forward with much anticipation to this new opportunity.

I woke up that Sunday morning and said good bye to my dad and Cory before starting the long drive to Nashville. As I pointed my old Chevy pickup truck westbound on I-40, I was both excited and nervous about starting the academy. I don't think it was butterflies in my stomach; rather it was a bunch of starving crocodiles fighting over a vulnerable wildebeest. I arrived in Nashville and had to stop for directions to the supply building so I could pick up everything I needed for the academy. I was supposed to arrive at the armory no later than 1200 hours and be at the academy by 1400 hours, ready to go.

When I finally finished getting all my gear I had just enough time to rush over to the training center so as not to be late. Pulling into to the parking, lot it became apparent how truly unprepared I was for what was coming next. All around me were men and women just like myself; the men with shaved heads. I stepped out of my truck and made small talk with some of them. This was the first time I had met any of my classmates. I was the only one from Monroe County hired for that class. After talking for a few minutes it was clear we all were wondering what the academy was going to be like. I had heard it was like basic training in the military, but having never served, I could only draw from what I had seen in movies and on TV.

Promptly at 1400 hours, Trooper (now Lieutenant) Robert Bighem, burst out of the gym and started yelling that we were late and we better hurry up and get inside and in formation. Not many of us really knew what that meant, but we sure tried (and failed miserably). As we ran into the gym the other instructors were also yelling and some classmates were already doing push-ups. I jumped in the first open spot I could find and stood at what I thought was attention (again, failing miserably). I must have done a fairly decent job since I only had to do a few push-ups for looking around at the others (a "no-no" while at attention).

The next twenty-four weeks proved to be some of the roughest I can recall. Being awakened at random times during the night for physical training (aka PT'd; a nice way of saying "run into the ground" while being put in a controlled stress environment) isn't what I had envisioned for academy. Oh, yeah, getting pepper sprayed wasn't all that much fun, either. I did more push-ups than I would have ever thought I could do. But, hey, that's what academy is for: to push you further than you think you can go. The goal is to instill in you the mantra, "You will go home at the end of your shift." A vital reason I am here today I owe to Lt. Bighem and the training staff at the THP academy. I really enjoyed working out and running after I got out of academy and stayed in good shape, using many of the exercise routines I learned while there.

Learning how to march and keep in step was probably my biggest challenge and what I ended up doing more push-ups for than anything else. I would often hear the lieutenant or one of the other instructors say something along the lines of, "Hey, Punchy, don't you know how to step? Give me ten push-ups! Maybe then you will learn how to step!" I was given the nickname "Punchy" because I always drank Hawaiian Punch instead of soda.

(Center) Recruit Lowell "Punchy" Russell with his Fruit Punch.

28

Somewhere around the fourteenth week of a six-month long academy the colonel came in to give us our tentative assignments (hopefully no one would wash out at this point). As he called out our names we would stand at attention as he told us where we would be assigned once we graduated. When he came to my name, he called out, "Recruit Russell, you are going to Marshall County. Do you know where that is?"

To which I replied, "Sir, no, sir."

To which he replied, "Well, there's a map on your desk."

There were some days that I wished I was home. The academy experience is tough and oftentimes frustrating while going through it, but great and rewarding once you have completed it. Although it was difficult, I am very glad I roughed it out, and I don't regret a bit of it.

Graduation day was awesome; August 10, 1998, will forever be a special day to me. My mom, dad, and brother were all there; it couldn't have been any better. Family has always meant everything to me. It was an unusually mild August day with a perfect temperature. We took a lot of pictures that I cherish to this day. While growing up our home was curiously absent of photos on the wall. I never really understood it, but I promised myself that in *my* home, memories would be available for all to see. If one were to come to my house they would see hundreds of photos on my walls, celebrating the highlights of life.

Field training was fairly uneventful. At the time, it was an eight-week program where you were assigned to a training officer who analyzed and graded you, giving you additional instruction along the way. Toward the end of the academy you were given time on the weekends to find a place to live in the area where you were assigned.

(L-R) Cory, Dad, Aunt Barbara, myself, and Aunt Linda at THP Academy graduation.

Since I didn't know anyone in Marshall County, I asked my lifelong friend, Charlie Swift, to make the trip there with me to look for a place to live. We found an apartment complex, and, lo and behold, there was already a trooper car parked there. I decided to pull in and introduce myself as the "new kid on the block" and see if this was a decent place to stay. I know it wasn't my first rookie error as a shaved-head, fresh-faced recruit to go knocking on a cop's door who didn't know me from Adam, and I know it wouldn't be my last. When he first opened the door I could tell he was on a heightened state of awareness, not knowing me. When I explained to him who I was and why I was there, I could tell by his look he was thinking, "Boy, you are crazy!" I didn't know Trooper Bob Logan before that day, but he showed himself to be a great Field Training Officer (FTO), and, thankfully, didn't flunk me!

After field training, I began my assignment with THP in Marshall County. Other than my fellow troopers I didn't really have many personal connections to the area. Although I was only three hours away from home it seemed like a thousand miles away. I was learning quickly that being a part of the highway patrol was going to be tougher than I had originally thought. I'm more of a hometown person, a homebody, and never really wanted to leave Monroe County. I also knew that if I wanted to fulfill my dream of being a state trooper I would have to be willing to live and move anywhere in the state.

My stint in Marshall County was fun and in due time I made a lot of friends. However, it was here that I had my first exposure with the hardest thing for law enforcement officers to face: the death of a fellow officer in the line of duty. My direct supervisor, Sergeant James Perry, called me a little before lunch and we had a short but pleasant conversation. As we were finishing up the call he said that he would see me that afternoon when I came on duty. When I went to work at 1500 hours I learned that not long after our conversation, while on a foot chase, Sgt. Perry had a heart attack and passed away. October 3, 1999 was a very sad day when I lost a friend and brother in blue, my first sergeant at the highway patrol.

Sgt. Perry's funeral was the very first law enforcement funeral that I had ever attended. Unfortunately, it wasn't the last. I was given the honor of being one of his pallbearers. Seeing his patrol car sitting next to his grave all polished up with tag number 7713 all ready to go was a very sobering reminder of how short life is and just how dangerous this job can be. You have to keep your body in good shape, not just your mind. As heartbreaking as it was to lose Sgt. Perry, the Lord used his death to continue to promote within me a desire to stay in good shape. In His own way, the Lord used Sgt. Perry's death to help me live through my future own moment of crisis! Twelve years later, when I would be preparing Frankie's funeral, the Lord recalled to my mind many of the things I learned through Sgt. Perry's funeral to apply to Frankie's. It truly is amazing how the Lord uses EVERYTHING we experience in life to help us in other moments of life.

Another area where this spiritual truth became evident was during the time I served in the Office of Professional Responsibility (OPR, aka Internal Affairs). I was assigned this position with my career long friend from academy, who now ranks as Lieutenant Stacey Wood-Heatherly. Stacey has been the best friend any human being could ask for. Our careers followed the same path from day one. We graduated academy together, we were promoted to sergeant together, and we also returned at nearly the same time to the Knoxville district from previous assignments.. We were two peas in a pod. Other than in the first couple of years, when we were given our first assignments straight out of academy, we have talked nearly every day.

In His own unique way, the Lord used a moment in Stacey's life to prepare me for the day Frankie would die. When her husband, Michael, (who is now a trooper as well) was deployed to Iraq with the Army, it brought many fears to surface within her. How would she handle it if she was notified of his death? How would she get to him overseas if he was wounded in combat? The lessons she learned *through her own experience* were passed to me, and helped to prepare me (as much as could be possible) for the day I was given notification of Frankie's death. Remember: *Everything* has a purpose with God.

After being posted in Marshall County from 1998-2000, I was transferred back to my home county. I served in Monroe County until March 2007, when I was promoted to sergeant in the OPR. I am thankful for how THP handles this position with true balance. It isn't a "good ol' boy network," where issues are merely swept under the rug or a "they're all guilty" approach where officers are constantly placed in fear of losing their jobs. It is one that desires to settle 100% on the facts and the truth.

With this position I did quite a bit of traveling around the state. I took advantage of my down time in my hotel rooms at the end of each day to finish my degree at Roane State Community College online. I had eighteen hours remaining and was able to complete them in short order. I worked in OPR until January 2011 when I was transferred back to District 1, Troop E, to work as the midnight shift supervisor in Knox and Union Counties. This is where I remained until the life-changing night of my crash.

Chaplain Grady often reminded me that everything God allows us to go through in life has a twofold purpose. One purpose is to strengthen us, and the other is to prepare us for what we will encounter later in life. The Bible teaches it in this manner in Romans 5:3-4: *"...knowing that tribulation worketh patience; And patience, experience; and experience, hope."* All the fiery trials I went through, even as a child, were preparing me for the next step; preparing me for the day my life would be changed forever. Humble Beginnings: the financial conditions of *my* childhood, *my* learning struggles, the divorce of *my* parents, all were tough things *I* had to endure to make *me* stronger and produce the kind of person that could "survive" academy, field training, and probation. It would also prepare *me* for the day *my* father died, to be followed by the time *my* mother died, and the day *my* close friend Frankie would be killed. All of this was preparing *me* for March 13, 2012.

Chapter 4
IT'S NOT JUST A J-O-B

"...For there is no power but of God: the powers that be are ordained of God."
Romans 13:1

I know that it has already been stated prior to this chapter, but I feel it bears repeating: Law enforcement is not just a job – it's a calling. The theme verse for this chapter even attests to this fact. Verse 4 of Romans 13 even says we (LEOs) are ministers of God! *"For he is the minister of God to thee for good. But if thou do that which is evil, be afraid; for he beareth not the sword in vain: for he is the minister of God, a revenger to execute wrath upon him that doeth evil."* Sure, it's an occupation, but it goes much deeper than that.

I worked many jobs when I was young that I didn't care for, and in fact, was quite happy when I was no longer doing them for a paycheck. Law enforcement is not among them. There have been many people that have come and gone from this profession, most having discovered it was not their calling. For those who are a part of "the called," the badge is a major part of their identity. This can be both a blessing and a curse at times. Just like anything else in life, law enforcement provides many memories – some good, some not so good. That's the job: the good, the bad, and the ugly.

One thing any officer will agree with me on while reading this book is how much we love talking about our job, especially with other LEOs. Please allow me to take a brief walk down my memory lane and break just the tip off the iceberg of a nearly twenty-year career full of memories. As I share with you my experiences, no doubt similar events of your own will come to mind.

Many of our childhood fantasy heroes had wings, capes, could fly, or were named after some form of a flying creature. You've heard of Batman and Robin, right? Well, I ask you: Have you ever heard of "Moth Boy?" In 1997, I was attending the Cleveland State Police Academy and working at the Monroe County Sheriff's Office on weekends. One evening, while on patrol, I had been tasked with serving a misdemeanor traffic warrant at a house in Tellico Plains. I stepped up on the porch to make contact and as we are taught, I was analyzing my surroundings. I noticed that the light on the porch didn't have a cover on it. Of course, with it being nearly dark and a warm night there were plenty of bugs flying around the lit bulb.

Standing slightly to one side of the door, I knocked. With the warrant in my left hand (always keep that shooting hand free!), while waiting for someone to come to the door, a moth decided that it would like to make my right ear canal his new home! Oh, did I mention that almost immediately upon knocking someone answered the door?! I was somehow able to mumble out my request to speak with the individual and was very happy when they told me he wasn't there. While up to this point I had been keeping my training in tact (not standing directly in front of a door, knowing my surroundings, keeping my gun hand free, etc…), I let all my training go out the window by not asking any further questions about the individual or his whereabouts. Instead, I managed to garble a "Thank you" and walked away promptly.

While still in the driveway, sitting in my cruiser, I was trying to work this buzzing pest out of my ear but to no avail! I sat there for at least two or three minutes while visions of the movie, *The Fly*, "flew" through my head. Recognizing quickly that I hadn't been trained for this, I decided the best course of action would be to drive to the Sweetwater Hospital and have a pro work his magic. When I got back to the academy the following Monday I shared the story with my fellow recruits and they decided to lovingly dub me "Moth Boy."

While I may be accused (and rightly so) of stating the obvious, there isn't a lot of love given to cops nowadays. Take a quick trip down memory lane and you will recall news stories involving law enforcement, and this truth becomes self-evident. For every positive story you remember about a LEO, I'm sure a conservative guess would show a 5-to-1 ratio for negative stories. The truth is, it only takes one officer doing the wrong thing to give the rest of us officers the proverbial black eye. The old saying is: "When I do good, no one remembers; when I do bad, no one forgets!" It's because of this mentality that we must take the opportunities the job gives us to make a positive impact on the lives of the people we serve. Sir Robert Peel did have some good philosophies. It's our duty to keep the public's image of law enforcement as clean as possible through positive interaction.

This takes me to a tragedy-turned-triumph memory. On August 29, 2001, I was dispatched to a motor vehicle accident (MVA) with injuries. It was one of the saddest moments of my career. A beautiful little girl, just shy of her eighth birthday, by the name of Brandi Watson had been killed in the accident. Brandi was a sweet girl, full of life and loved by everyone she knew. She didn't know a stranger, treating everyone she met like they were family. Brandi loved playing outdoors and had a special talent for playing baseball. She was best friends with her sister, Brittany. Brittany is much like her sibling, having a love for sports and flourishing as a basketball player.

Monroe County Captain Travis Jones and I on scene at the crash that killed Brandi Watson.

There are moments in life that can make you a better person. For me, this was one of them. It grieved me to see an innocent, defenseless life that I couldn't help. As much as it hurt, I knew the pain was much deeper for the family. I couldn't help her, but I could help them. I knew the father, Randy, who was a member of the Monroe County Rescue Squad (MCRS) I would later meet the rest of the family after the crash. I've always had a tremendous amount of respect for the men and women of the MCRS and other squads that volunteer to put themselves in the way of danger for those in need. The Watsons were a good family that just had their lives changed and they needed help.

Over the next several months I called the family every few days to ask how they were doing and would stop by on occasion just to spend time with them. I didn't realize until later how big of an impact this made on the family. A special side note blessing during this time happened when I was able to make contact with Brittany's hero, Pat Summitt, the legendary former University of Tennessee Lady Vols basketball coach. She gave me a personalized, autographed photo to give to her. Coach Summitt's thoughtful gesture went a long way to help Brittany in the healing process with the death of her sister.

A few days after the wreck I drove past the location of the accident and noticed where friends and family had put up a cross and flowers. I stopped at a local florist and picked up some flowers to also put at the scene. Moments like these have taught me that a little act of kindness can go a long way. While I wasn't able to attend Brandi's funeral service, I've made it a personal goal to try to attend the funeral of any

39

vehicle fatality I've worked in my career to support the families in their time of grief.

One of the most rewarding days of my career was January 28, 2010. It was shortly after midnight and I was sitting in a church parking lot off of I-75, exit 76, while working on some paperwork. It was a quiet place that I could focus on the task at hand. I had just come back to the road after being off for four years serving in the OPR unit. It was a pleasure to serve in that capacity for a time, but nevertheless, I was glad to be back on the road.

As I was working, a "be on the lookout" (BOLO) came over the radio out of Monroe County for a gold, 1996 Toyota Camry. The county dispatch received a distress call from a female who stated she had been assaulted and placed in the trunk of the vehicle. Dispatch advised they could be headed toward I-75. Since I was only approximately a mile away I drove up onto the ramp where I could set up and observe traffic. Within just a few minutes a vehicle matching the description passed my position.

I pulled out behind the vehicle and radioed THP dispatch to verify the tag. When it was confirmed that this was in fact the Camry in question, I requested assistance from troopers a few miles up ahead to prepare for a felony traffic stop. The information was also passed forward to the Knox County Sheriff's Office and the Knoxville Police Department. When the realization hit me that I hadn't made a felony stop in over four years, the "butterflies" started in my stomach. As my muscle memory kicked in I was then thankful for the excellent training I received at the Cleveland

State and THP Academies. As we neared the outskirts of Knoxville at the I-75/I-40 split, I (along with three additional troopers) conducted the felony traffic stop. Thankfully, for all involved we were able to detain the suspect and rescue the kidnap victim. By the time we had stopped the vehicle she had been taken out of the trunk and placed in the front seat. All is well that ends well.

The first time I had the opportunity to work with Chaplain Grady, the co-author, came in another tragedy-turned-triumph story. On November 26, 2011, a twenty-year-old young man by the name of Kyle Anito made a bad mistake. Kyle was a good kid growing up, never giving his parents any problems. He decided one night to break the rules and it cost him dearly. Kyle went to a party where there was alcohol, and while he had not planned on drinking, he later succumbed to peer pressure. His objective was to safely drive home those who had been drinking. After he began consuming alcohol (knowing he shouldn't), Kyle then made plans with another buddy to drive him home. Later in the night his ride left the party while he was still there. When Kyle was ready to leave he still had no intention of driving himself home. However, some of his "friends" helped him walk to the car, opened the door, and even buckled him in because he was too inebriated to do it himself.

In those early morning hours, I was sitting at the THP office speaking to a dispatcher and gathering information from the previous shift. A call came over the radio from one of the troopers that he was in pursuit of a vehicle (Kyle's). He had been clocked driving 79 MPH in a 40 MPH zone. When the trooper activated his lights, Kyle took off in an attempt to evade the trooper instead of pulling over. When the pursuit took a turn onto a curvy road Kyle lost control of the car and hit a tree, the impact killing him. The car caught fire with him inside. Chaplain Grady was called to the scene and from there he and I and another trooper went to the home of Tim and Terri Anito for what would be one of the most difficult death notifications ever made in my career.

It was still the early hours of the morning and the sun was just beginning to rise as we arrived at their house. When Mr. Anito opened the door you could discern from the look on his face that he knew something bad had happened, just not what. It was as if we were watching his world turn upside down as we told him the news no parent ever wants to hear. In turn, we had to notify Kyle's sisters who at the time were still sleeping. Mrs. Anito was out Christmas shopping as it was "Black Friday" weekend, thus requiring the notification to be made once again. We also aided the family in notifying additional kin and securing their ministerial support.

Through this great tragedy a beautiful thing was born. Tim Anito has traveled all through the state of Tennessee speaking to youth about many subjects that came out of that night, subjects such as: making good decisions, individual responsibility, underage drinking, and the dangers of drinking and driving. What a special man Tim is – he never placed the blame on the trooper for his son's actions. He took a horrible life-altering event and turned it into an opportunity to help other families to (hopefully) avoid the same events that came to their home that fateful morning.

As you can see from these select stories, *It's Not Just a J-O-B*. There will be highs to hang your hat on at the end of the shift. There will also be lows that are an equal part of the job that you endure for the betterment of the people you serve. If you are an officer, take a moment to reflect on your experiences: Did you leave anything undone? What can you do better? Find what motivates you to do this job well and cling to it. You won't go wrong, I guarantee it. Remember, this job isn't for everybody, it's a calling!

Investigating a fatal crash on Hwy 360 in Vonore, TN.

Chapter 5

THE VALLEY OF THE SHADOW OF DEATH

"When my father and my mother forsake me, then the LORD will take me up."

Psalm 27:10

After Mom and Dad's divorce it took a while for things to resemble some form of familial normalcy. While Mom went back to living in Blount County (the next county over) and Cory and I had chosen to stay with Dad in Monroe County, there was no estrangement between children and parents. As we grew into adulthood, we learned to love them both more every day, despite the divorce.

The year 2009 was the beginning of a four-year whirlwind of wild events. Dad had been sick for a few years at this point with Chronic Obstructive Pulmonary Disease (COPD) and other respiratory issues, but the symptoms were fairly controlled. Occasionally, Dad would have to be admitted into the hospital for treatment but beyond that all was well. A boy named Frankie Watson (you'll learn more about him in the next chapter) had come to live with us, and on the days that I was working in OPR out of town, Dad would get him up and make sure he was getting ready for school. Each morning when I would call to check on

Frankie, Dad and I would have a good time talking on the phone. Things seemed pretty normal; everything was business as usual.

In late October, Dad was having some issues with his COPD, so he was transported by ambulance to Sweetwater Hospital. While there, his COPD became so severe, the doctor felt it would be a better fit for him to move to a hospital that was more suited to assist his particular need. He was transported to Parkwest Medical Center in Knoxville for treatment. While there, dad started having pains in his abdomen. The doctor decided to run a dye test and noticed an obstruction in his bowels. He then ordered a scope to be run to determine the size of the obstruction. Dad was in immense pain and needed this complication corrected as soon as possible.

During the scope something went tragically wrong. It wasn't an issue of medical malpractice but rather that Dad had weakened bowels. While undergoing the procedure his bowels ruptured. The end result was a release of toxins into his blood stream, an event called sepsis. While in much pain, thankfully, for his sake it didn't last long. Dad died on November 5, 2009, sadly memorable as the day of the first Fort Hood shooting. Larry Russell was only fifty-eight years old

While, yes, I was a full-grown man in my thirties, this was a low blow to me. I loved my dad. We were close like a father and son should be. At the time of his death, I was a supervisor in OPR, and when home, would normally leave for work around 0600 hours. I would call Dad every morning on my way to work and help make sure Frankie was

(L-R) Myself, Dad, and Cory.

up and getting ready for school, but mainly just to spend some time talking with him on the phone. I loved those times where I could just release from the pressures of work and talk to him about nothing. I wouldn't have traded those moments for anything.

The next few months after Dad's death were hard when I was driving to work and did not have that father-son phone call with which to prepare for the day. This grieving process was interrupted just four short months later when I received an unexpected phone call. Cory was on the other end of the line telling me I needed to head to the Blount Memorial Hospital ASAP. Mom had suffered a brain aneurysm and was unresponsive but still alive. Just as with my dad's situation, the doctor at Blount Memorial recommended that my mother be moved to the University of Tennessee Hospital, which had an advanced trauma unit that could better help her situation. She was immediately placed on life support and tests were started to analyze just how bad the brain bleed was. A couple of days later the doctor came to us with the results of the tests. It didn't appear Mom would recover. An odd coincidence would be that her aneurysm occurred exactly two years prior to the day of my on-duty accident.

This was just as big of a shock to Cory and me as Dad's situation was. We definitely did not see this coming. Like Dad, Mom had some minor health issues, but nothing that would lead us to this conclusion. Prior to this event she had been diagnosed with early-onset Alzheimer's but had been dealing with it well, having only an occasional symptom show itself.

My brother and I now faced a difficult decision: Do we leave her on life support, basically brain dead and hoping for a miracle, or do we take her off and end her suffering? From an outsider's perspective when just looking at the facts, it's a conclusion that the medical professional may have an easier time making, but it's a whole different ball game when you are talking about the one who brought you into the world. My mother's pastor, who was also my childhood pastor, George Macht, was there to help us through this difficult situation. I was thankful for his presence and support during this trying time when we made the decision to take her off life support. Shirley Russell died on March 16, 2010, at the age of fifty-five. Frankie was in the room with us at each hospital when Mom and Dad died and served as a pallbearer for both funerals.

Mom's death was particularly difficult to deal with because we were still dealing with Dad's passing. Both parents dying relatively young, back-to-back and unexpectedly was a lot to process for sure! There had to be something to this, not just a coincidence. Later on down the road the Lord showed me a special verse in the Scriptures. Psalm 27:10 says, *"When my father and my mother forsake me, then the LORD will take me up."* I had just lost both of my parents, but the Lord was about to reveal Himself to me in a special and unique way (see Chapter 7). God promised in His word that when the ones you love, trust, and lean on the most depart, He will be there for you. He promised He would never leave you nor forsake you (Deuteronomy 31:6-8; Hebrews 13:5).

Mom and I at my graduation from THP Academy, August 10, 1998.

As I mentioned earlier in Chapter 3, the Lord will use trials like this to prepare you for future events in life. Everyone wants an easy, problem-free life; however, problems and trials are a guarantee of the human condition. The Bible has a lot to say about this. A couple of passages that pretty much sum up life this side of eternity are Job 5:7, *"Yet man is born unto trouble, as the sparks fly upward,"* and Job 14:1, *"Man that is born of a woman is of few days, and full of trouble."* We shouldn't be shocked when something bad happens to us, thinking that bad things always happen to someone else. We are assured by God's word that bad things happen to every person in life, both good and bad. Matthew 5:45 unequivocally states this fact: *"That ye may be the children of your Father which is in heaven: for he maketh his sun to rise on the evil and on the good, and sendeth rain on the just and on the unjust."*

The difference in perspective is that, as children of God, we have special promises others don't. One promise is that He will be there for us in our trials and tribulations. What a blessed thought that God is with us through it all. The second promise is how the Lord will turn the bad into good for His children. In Romans 8:28 we receive this special blessing: *"And we know that all things work together for good to them that love God, to them who are the called according to his purpose."* Stand up to the trials you are faced with, take courage and meet them head on with God. Don't let your trials define you, rather you define them. If you are God's child, you have the strongest power in your corner to help you come out victorious. Stand strong and see what God can do. He's preparing you for the next stage of your life. Everything that happened to this point in my life God was using to prepare me for what was going to happen the next year. I had not yet completed the journey through *The Valley of the Shadow of Death.*

Chapter 6

FRANKIE

"Finally, my brethren, be strong in the Lord, and in the power of his might."
Ephesians 6:10

Life often takes unexpected turns: sometimes for the good, sometimes for the bad. It's like the analogy of canoeing on a winding river – you don't know what's around the bend until you get there. Every so often the current picks up and things get a little rocky, and on other occasions all is quiet and serene. Such would be the case in the unique relationship I would build with Franklin "Frankie" Namon Watson. I first met him in 2002 when he was just a young, scrappy, twelve-year-old boy, and was privileged to watch him grow up to be an exceptional young man. Little did I know just how much of an impact he would later have in my life.

Frankie lived in the small nearby community of Sweetwater. Between 2002 and 2004, I would only see him occasionally, either around town or when he was at his grandparent's house. He always seemed like a decent kid and was pleasant to be around. During the summer of 2004, I had set up a fireworks stand in Madisonville in anticipation of the upcoming 4th of July celebrations. Frankie stopped by and while we were chatting he asked me if I could take him to his football practices on the days that his dad was unable. I told him as long as his folks didn't mind I would be happy to drive him. When the football team began having two practices a day Frankie would spend the night. Dad and I lived in a large house that had a spare bedroom where he would stay. I would take him to the morning practices when I wasn't working and Dad was happy to take him on the days I did work. Just like that, Frankie was becoming a special part of our lives.

Frankie's dedication showed early on in life with his hard work on the football field.

It didn't take long for a familial-like relationship to blossom. Frankie was like a little brother to me and grew to be an integral part of the family. I surmise that this was because I saw myself in Frankie when I was his age. I remembered Coach Evans taking an interest in me and how I used to stay the night at his house and how they "adopted" me into their family. I saw in Frankie a young man with a world of potential, and I had the opportunity to be an influence in his life. I wasn't going to waste that opportunity. Hardly any time passed before he was traveling with us on family vacations and special outings. I told him I would take him anywhere he wanted to go for his senior trip and he chose to go to Hawaii. It was one of the best trips we ever took.

One of my favorite memories of Frankie was Christmas 2005. I purchased a paintball gun for him, and boy, you would have thought a brand new Ferrari was parked out front! Frankie invited his buddy, Michael Elliot, to spend the night. Later that afternoon I went downstairs to do some laundry and noticed they weren't in his room. When I went back upstairs I asked Dad if he knew where they were. He just kind of chuckled and said that I should try looking out the window. When I did, I initially wasn't sure what to do. Standing out in the freezing cold were two teenage boys, shirtless, taking turns shooting each other with the paintball gun! When I asked them what possessed them to do this, in all his teenage wisdom Frankie advised me that they just wanted to see how big of a welt it would leave! While having a hard time regaining my composure from having laughed myself into tears, I put an end to the shenanigans and sent the boys back inside. The next incident with the paintball gun was when I found paintballs in my freezer. After confiscating the paintballs I asked him if there was any good purpose for why they were in there, to which he simply replied that he was preparing for a paintball war. Yes, even the best of kids are still just that – kids!

(L-R) Frankie, Michael Elliot, and myself at their high school graduation, May 2008.

Frankie was a young man full of life; he didn't waste a moment. At times, that spirit had the ability to breed a little mentality of mischievousness (as can be seen in the previous story). I had been in Nashville for work the last couple of days and was coming back into town for the weekend. I told Frankie as soon as I got in I would need to take a quick shower and change before we could leave to go out for dinner. Later, as I was putting on my deodorant, the phone rang. While talking on the phone I went to Frankie's room to see if he was ready. About the time I hit his room my armpits started to tingle, then burn! I didn't know why, but Frankie was laughing at me. By the time I hung up the phone my armpits felt as if they had pepper spray on them! In desperation I asked him what was going on, and in between his bursts of laughter he told me he had put *Icy Hot* on my deodorant! We had a good laugh about it (obviously he more than me).

I accidentally got my revenge a couple of years later. Frankie joined the Marines and while in boot camp he had developed a bad rash on his legs. He sent a letter back requesting help with the matter. Having been single my whole life and not having any children of my own, I wasn't sure what to do. I called my wonderful sister-in-law, Crystal, and asked for her advice. She recommended I buy some extra strength *Desitin* to send to him. I went to the store, bought the product and mailed it to him along with a note taped to the product, explaining the instructions. I don't remember exactly what I said in the note, but it was something like this: "Rub a generous portion of cream on the infected areas and apply as frequently as necessary." At the time I didn't realize all incoming mail was inspected prior to being given to the respective designee. It took him a while to live down that "care package."

Ever since he was a little child Frankie had expressed an interest in being a police officer and/or Marine. He graduated from high school in May of 2008 and immediately started into his law enforcement career as a corrections officer at the Monroe County Sheriff's Office. In 2009, he went to the Cleveland State Police Academy and was hired on to the Madisonville Police Department that December. In 2010, he enlisted in the Marines and was sent to Parris Island for boot camp. He was deployed to Afghanistan in 2011. Frankie was a combat engineer and had earned the rank of Lance Corporal (LCpl). His long-term ambition was to become a Tennessee State Trooper after he returned from his deployment.

(L-R) Myself, Gov. Bill Haslam, wife Crissy, and Frankie Watson enjoying a moment.

This is where the next bend in the river revealed violent rapids. On Saturday, September 24, 2011, Frankie was killed by an enemy sniper while on foot patrol in a corn field outside his forward operating base (FOB). He was only

Frankie at Paris Island.

twenty-one years old. By this point in our nine-year relationship Frankie felt close enough to my family, that he listed me, in addition to his parents, Troy Watson and Stacy Couch, as next of kin to be notified in case of death or injury.

That morning I got off work at 0700 hours and had gone to bed. I had to be up in just a few hours for an overtime assignment. I awoke around noon and hopped in the shower to get ready for the day. I was in the shower when the Marines first came to give me the death notification. They didn't know I was a trooper and, having seen my cruiser in the driveway, thought I had already been notified by THP. Unaware they had come to the house, I continued getting ready and drove up into Knoxville. About the time I arrived at the truck scales, I received a radio call informing me I needed to go back home. When I arrived back at the house, the Marine detail was already there, waiting for me to return.

Pictures of Frankie serving his country in Afghanistan.

Sitting on my couch in my living room, I felt a world of emotions go through me as they notified me of Frankie's death. Immediately word spread and people started coming from all over to offer their condolences. My brother was one of the most welcomed faces to see. After having lost my mother, father, and now Frankie, Cory remained my only immediate living relative and these moments have served to draw us closer than ever. I thank God for my brother.

You never know how the Lord plans to work. Out of this horrific event many lasting friendships have blossomed. This was the first time I met my partner in this book, Chaplain Grady. I remember him coming by that day, but I was in such a fog that it didn't really hit me until I saw him again at the funeral, just exactly who he was. Over the next few months we would exchange several texts and phone calls and become friends, eventually crossing paths on the job from time to time.

A wise old preacher once said, "Don't make a decision, when your decision maker is broken." In times of duress, it is wise to find someone you can look to for help. During this tumultuous event, that someone for me was United States Air Force Captain James Brantley. Captain Brantley had been a friend to us for many years, and a mentor to Frankie. He had been stationed at Vance Air Force Base in Oklahoma, when he received the news of Frankie's death. A close mutual friend of ours, Mr. Bill Talman (my flight instructor), helped to keep Captain Brantley up to date when I was unreachable. Captain Brantley put his work on hold to fly straight to Dover Air Force Base in order to be there for the family, and guide us through the challenging time that lay ahead for us. When the time came to bring Frankie home from Dover, Captain Brantley headed up the military escort. Mr. Todd Rose, Chief of Air Force Mortuary Affairs, was instrumental in placing Captain Brantley on official orders for Frankie's detail. The Fisher House Foundation was a huge blessing to the family throughout the whole process. Thank God for men of sacrifice – men like Frankie and Captain Brantley.

Frankie's homecoming, funeral and graveside services were nothing short of breathtaking. Vehicles and thousands of people lined the shoulders of Highway 411 and saluted him as his escort arrived in town. His funeral service was packed to overflowing in the 800-plus seat auditorium of the First Baptist Church in Madisonville, Tennessee, with several dignitaries in attendance. There were over 2,000 people that watched the service via the internet. They had to place the service on a special out-of-state server with another one as a backup. Frankie was given full honors, which he had so deservedly earned. In April 2013, Highway 411 in Madisonville was dedicated in memory of Frankie and renamed the "Franklin "Frankie" Watson Memorial Highway."

Frankie was a devoted Christian man. While he was overseas, he had personal, daily devotions using his Bible along with a devotional book his friends, Allyson Mason and Caleb Bowers, had given him. An impressive demonstration pointing to his character was a verse he posted on his Facebook page before leaving for Afghanistan. Fittingly, this same verse was also inscribed as part of the epitaph on his tombstone. Joshua 1:9: *"Have not I*

60

commanded thee? Be strong and of a good courage; be not afraid, neither be thou dismayed: for the LORD thy God is with thee whithersoever thou goest."

Visiting Frankie's grave.

An equally impressive passage of Scripture that "speaks" to this topic is Hebrews 11:4: *"...he being dead yet speaketh."* When Frankie died I vowed I wouldn't let his memory die with him. I founded a memorial scholarship fund in Frankie's honor. Today there are several young folks

61

who have been given the opportunity to attend college because of his sacrifice. (See the "About the LCpl Frankie Watson Memorial Scholarship Fund" in the appendix.) In addition to the fund, I travel as often as I am able to speak to veterans groups, law enforcement academies, and similar functions to honor the life and sacrifice of Frankie.

I have no doubt that you, the reader, have by now observed the recurring theme of how God uses things in your past to *prepare* you for the future. Just as God used *me* in Frankie's life, He used <u>*Frankie*</u> in mine. My parents' unexpected deaths worked to *prepare* me for Frankie's unexpected death and also to motivate me to what I do today. He also used Frankie's death in addition to my parent's deaths, to *prepare* me for my day. He allowed me to walk through the valley of the shadow of death three times to *prepare* me for walking through my own valley. As we were taught in law enforcement: *"Preparation* is the key to survival. When the time for decision arrives, the time for *preparation* is past."* After Frankie's funeral, the waters of the river seemed to calm. The rapids would return 5 ½ short months later as the river entered my valley. *Preparation* time was over. My valley of decision had arrived.

My favorite picture of Frankie and me – "Lest we forget."

Chapter 7
THE JAILOR'S STORY

"And brought them out, and said, Sirs, what must I do to be saved?"

Acts 16:30

When my mother went into the hospital, I felt a little vulnerable. While on the job, I saw death on a regular basis; this time it was hitting right at home with one parent dead and the other about to die. Even having Pastor Macht there to comfort and help, something still wasn't right. Something was missing. As I stood there looking at my precious, fragile, mother clinging helplessly to life this side of eternity, my heart ached. I loved my mother. I was very close to her my whole life. I was having some really, dark, personal struggles knowing that once she died, that was it. I would put her in the ground; I wouldn't see her again.

But, wait! While standing there the redeeming truth of Proverbs 22:6 came to life: *"Train up a child in the way he should go: and when he is old, he will not depart from it."* I was raised in a Christian home with Judeo-Christian values gently, and at times, not so gently guiding me. I learned about the Gospel of Jesus Christ at a young age, but had never submitted myself to it.

Allow me to deviate for just a moment from my story to talk to you about the most important personal aspect of my life – the Gospel of Jesus Christ. Quite often, when we as human beings get ahold of something, we unnecessarily overcomplicate it. I have learned that the greatest news ever delivered to man has fallen prey to this same practice. As a law enforcement officer I found the Gospel almost "too good to be true," hence, kicking in the jaded, skeptical attitude that quite often comes with the job.

In I Corinthians 15:1-4, the Apostle Paul laid out the basic components of the Gospel. He said: *"Moreover, brethren, **I declare unto you the gospel** which I preached unto you, which also ye have received, and wherein ye stand; By which also ye are saved, if ye keep in memory what I preached unto you, unless ye have believed in vain. For I delivered unto you first of all that which I also received, how that **Christ died for our sins** according to the scriptures; And that **he was buried**, and that **he rose again the third day** according to the scriptures."*

The rudimentary definition of the word gospel is "good news." According to the Scriptures, the best news ever delivered to man is that Christ died for our sins, was buried, and on the third day rose from the dead, victorious over death, hell, and the grave. Christ did all this for you and me. Foolishly, I had faced death many times on the job without letting the truth of the Gospel settle upon my heart. That changed the day before my mother's death. Ironically, it was almost two years to the day I almost died.

As a law enforcement officer, one of the most beautiful things the Lord ever showed me is how He used an officer of the law – a corrections officer to be exact – to ask the most important question in human history. In Acts 16, the Apostle Paul was wrongfully thrown into prison. While he and Silas were having a little dose of "jailhouse religion," the Lord worked a miracle. An earthquake broke open all the doors of the jail. The jailor, fearing a mass escape and knowing it would mean he would be held accountable with his own life for the loss of prisoners, was about to commit suicide. Paul spoke up and stopped him, telling him that all the prisoners were accounted for. When the jailor saw the awesome power of God it humbled him, leading him to ask the most profound question ever: *"What must I do to be saved?"* The only thing more profound and eternal than the question was the answer: *"Believe on the Lord Jesus Christ, and thou shalt be saved."*

Did you notice the little but important word *on*? There have been many people who have come and gone believing *in* Jesus but never believing *on* Jesus. *In* means you believe that Jesus is God in a corporate sense. *On* means it is personal, something that you accept as your own. Growing up, I had heard the preacher many times tell me that Gospel truth; Jesus died for my sins, was buried, and rose again the third day. If I would personally accept Him as my Saviour, then I would be saved; no ifs, ands, or buts about it! I wouldn't have to fear death or hell. I would have eternal victory in the Gospel of Jesus Christ. However, up to the point where I was standing at my dying mother's hospital bed, I had only believed *in* Jesus Christ. I had grown up believing He was God in the flesh. I believed He died, was buried, and rose from the dead. Even so, I had never taken the time to make it personal. Standing there at her deathbed, I thought to myself, "I want to see my mother again and there is only *one* way that will happen."

Leaving her bedside, I went downstairs to the first floor, just outside the emergency room (the same emergency room where I would be fighting for my life just two short years later) with Pastor Macht to talk with him about it. He shared with me this Gospel message which I was already familiar with. Finally, it clicked: This is what had been missing! The *on* part had never happened for me! Standing right there, I prayed to God and asked Him to save me. I knew there was not enough good in me or in my life to earn eternal life. Later, when we took my mother off life support and she passed away, I knew that this wouldn't be the end. When I walked away from her bedside for the last time, I walked away a child of God. I walked away knowing I would see my mother again. I walked away having believed *on* the Lord. A short time later, the thought would hit me, "If I had died on the job before today, I would be in hell!" What a peace it was to my soul when I did as the Philippian jailer did 2,000 years ago and called *upon* the name of the Lord.

What a blessing to know God has been saving cops for that long and He still is today. The most powerful *truth* about the Gospel from a cop's perspective is to know it addresses the "trust" issue we carry as our everyday baggage. Just get lied to a dozen times a day for a living and see how hard it is to trust someone. Notwithstanding, the Bible says in Romans 3:4, "...let **God be true**, *but every man* *a liar…"* He also said in John 14:6, *"…I am the way, **the truth**, and the life…"* Most things in life that seem "too good to be true" usually are. The *truth* of the Gospel is this: God did the hard part – dying for your sins – because He loved you, His creation. He made your part in salvation as simple as calling **upon** Him to save you. Our job as officers is to discern the *truth*. The *truth* is that God and His word are *truth* and He said He would save you if you would call **on** Him. I would encourage everyone, officer or not, as in <u>The Jailor's Story,</u> if you have never taken the time to believe **on** the Lord, may today be that day. And on a side note, we as officers like to have eye witnesses, right? Well, after giving us the Gospel definition in I Corinthians 15:1-4, the Lord listed over 500 eye witnesses to His resurrection in verses 5-8. How's that for evidence?!

My baptism with Dr. Lon Shoopman.

Chapter 8
AN OPEN DOOR

"... These things saith he that is holy, he that is true, ... he that openeth, and no man shutteth ... I know thy works: behold, I have set before thee an open door, and no man can shut it ..."
Revelation 3:7-8

When recounting the events of March 13, 2012, one can be nothing less than amazed; not necessarily amazed at what happened to me in those early morning hours and the days that followed, but at the power and glory of God that was to be revealed. The scene of the accident looked like something out of a war zone. I was, by all human accounts, supposed to die – not just one way, but many ways. Let me tell you the story.

It was roughly 0250 hours and I had just finished a traffic stop on I-40 inside the city limits of Knoxville. It was a cool, late winter morning as I sat on the shoulder of the interstate alone, having already released the driver from the stop. I was making notes on the citation for court when the accident occurred. Pretty much everything that happened to me from that moment through the next several days was relayed to me secondhand.

While working on the citation with my emergency lights still activated, a flatbed semi-truck veered out of its lane, striking the back of my cruiser. The impact threw my car several hundred feet forward and into a tailspin, eventually ending up against the inside barrier wall on the opposite side of the west-bound lanes. It was later discovered that the driver, Mr. Eric Lewis of FSH Trucking Co. in Orlando, Florida, had fallen asleep at the wheel of his rig. He was traveling from Pennsylvania to Texas with a load of construction equipment. I will discuss more about him in the next chapter.

Almost immediately, my car burst into flames. Here is where you begin to see the providential hand of the Lord intervening. Chief David Rausch of the Knoxville Police Department was quoted by the Knoxville News Sentinel (see Appendix for link to article) as saying this about the event: "As we say time and again – divine intervention. It's a game of seconds. If neither the officers or the paramedics had been in the area, we would have had a much more tragic situation."

Within mere seconds of the impact, an ambulance from McMinn County (approximately an hour away from Knoxville) was returning to Athens, Tennessee, after transporting a patient to a Knoxville-area hospital. As the ambulance crested a rise in the road, the driver, Paramedic Freddie Leslie, and his partner, Kristi Graham, spotted my cruiser as it was still spinning toward the inside wall! They came to a stop on scene almost at the same time the cruiser was coming to a halt. How's that for divine intervention?!

70

According to the details from the investigation listed in the crash report, the impact had knocked me nearly a football field in length from where I had been sitting. Mr. Lewis, the truck driver, brought his truck to a stop as quickly as possible; even then it took over 1,000 feet to accomplish the task. He also came running to my aid as the paramedics arrived. It was as if God was saying, "I've got you covered from all angles, son. Now, watch this!" A Knoxville Police Department (KPD) K-9 Officer, Andrew Keith, had been en route to assist another officer on a vehicle search when he came up on the wreck, also within seconds. He was on scene mere moments after the others and was able to call for additional assistance from the Knoxville Fire Department (KFD), KPD, THP, and Rural Metro Ambulance Services.

Freddie and Mr. Lewis both tugged at my door and it popped open. While exhausting two fire extinguishers and starting on a third to keep the flames back, they worked frantically to free me, but my seatbelt had pulled tight from the impact. Dennis Stevens, a painter who had been working at the nearby Sam's Club, was just leaving work and stopped to help. He "just so happened" to have a box cutter on him that he used to begin cutting me free. He and Officer Keith, using his own knife, worked together to cut me loose from the seatbelt just as the flames started spreading. Running out of time, with one last-ditch effort, Freddie pulled me by my left leg, loosing me from the car. Officer Keith, Freddie, and the others were able to pull me from the vehicle and begin CPR. Just seconds after, my seat was fully engulfed in flames.

Shortly after Officer Keith's arrival on scene, KPD

Officer Steve Taylor arrived to assist in my aide. He had seen me earlier, while I was on my traffic stop, and was able to quickly return to the scene of the wreck when the radio call for help went out. His lone act may have made the difference in my survival. As Freddie and Kristi were performing CPR on me on the ground while awaiting Rural Metro for transport, the ammunition in what was left of my trunk began to explode. Officer Taylor jumped into the ambulance and drove it between us and the burning cruiser so as to shield the paramedics and myself from harm.

So many people quickly fell into place in such an extraordinary fashion. KPD Officer Fred Kimber could be heard on the radio coordinating traffic control along with the other officers. KFD quickly arrived to extinguish the flames. Rural Metro brought me safely to the emergency room where the Lord worked miracles in the days to come through the doctors and nurses at the University of Tennessee Hospital. He worked through my various therapists, not to mention the thousands of prayers from all around the world. Even after being delivered from my burning cruiser I was not out of danger. I would remain on life support for fourteen days before being stable enough to have my first of two neck and spinal surgeries.

Before we proceed further with the story, let's look at how I should have died:

1.   **Impact** – The impact was so severe that it crushed a Ford Crown Victoria to about half its normal size. It was estimated that the semi was traveling at approximately sixty-nine miles per hour at the point of impact. The whiplash

alone from the impact should have destroyed my organs and spinal column.

2.	**Fire** – I should have been consumed in the fire. Period.

3.	**Ammunition** – Hundreds of rounds of live ammunition that were in the trunk were igniting in the fire and exploding.

4.	**Fractured Skull and Broken Neck/Back** – My skull fractured at the base of my neck. This type of fracture can lead to the spine puncturing the brain and ending life as we know it. I survived this injury. My neck and back suffered multiple fractures.

5.	**Infection** – Due to the massive trauma my body endured, I had to receive large quantities of antibiotics to stay alive. One infection was cleaned up only for another to try and take its place. There was a fear of pneumonia at one point, although, thankfully, it never did take hold.

6.	**Smoke Inhalation** – I had damage to my lungs from the black smoke emitted from my cruiser while trapped inside the inferno.

Although I don't really remember anything from the crash itself, I do have several memories from the previous twenty-four hours. Less than 48 hours before I was to work the last shift I would ever have in a patrol car, I had been interviewed by Dylan Belcher, a student at Sequoyah High School, for a term paper he was doing on law enforcement. Ironically, I had told him that law enforcement officers were more likely to be killed in a car crash than by any other means.

I remember preparing for work that day, an overtime assignment bringing me in early. I had been reflecting on Frankie's time as a police officer as I walked into my room and looked at my gear. As I was standing there looking at the brass, the badge, the patch, and admiring the uniform that I had worked hard for and tried my best to honor, an uncanny thought popped into my head: "I wonder how many officers killed in the line of duty knew within themselves that day would be their last time putting on the uniform." Although I remember the thought, I don't remember working the overtime assignment.

The last memory I have prior to going on shift was that I had decided I wanted to spend some time at Frankie's grave. I was missing him a little extra, and maybe you could call me melancholy, but it was just one of several oddities from the day. After paying my respects, I stopped at a local McDonald's to get myself a large, "healthy" *Hi-C*. I had planned to meet up with my friend, Alcoa Police Officer, Dustin "Cookie" Cook. We had a good time chatting for about 15 minutes before I took off to go on patrol. I remember meeting with Cookie, but I can't recall the conversation.

Dylan's interview, Frankie's grave, my own thoughts…coincidence? Some may say, yes. I believe somewhere deep down in my heart the Lord was preparing me for what was coming around the bend. In Isaiah 55:8 the Bible says, *"For my thoughts are not your thoughts, neither are your ways my ways, saith the LORD.*" I don't know exactly what the Lord wanted to accomplish through the memories he allowed me to retain from that day. However, the thought I have is that the Lord knew what I needed for my strength while lying in the hospital bed. These memories provided mental and emotional strength for me during my recovery.

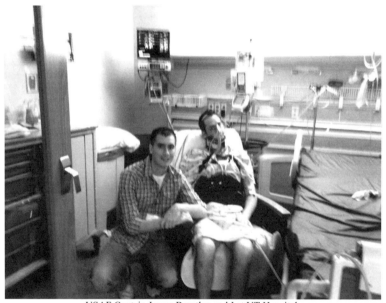

USAF Captain James Brantley and I at UT Hospital.

One thing I do know is that while the days following were very hard to accept, I found the words of Christ first given to the Apostle Paul in his time of affliction rang more and more true each passing day. II Corinthians 12:9 says, *"And he said unto me, My grace is sufficient for thee: for my strength is made perfect in weakness. Most gladly therefore will I rather glory in my infirmities, that the power of Christ may rest upon me."* If I was to glory in my infirmities, the

Lord gave me much to glory in! Here is a medical and layman's language breakdown of just some of the trauma visited upon my body:

- Atlanto-Occipital Dislocation (Internal Decapitation) – My skull detached from the spinal column. This is a rare phenomenon with a high mortality rate.
- Basilar Skull Fracture – My skull fractured at the base, which can cause the bottom of the brain to be impaled on the spinal cord. Many famous race car drivers have died from this type of injury.
- Multiple fractures in my neck and back.
- 8 ribs were fractured or broken.
- Lacerated liver.
- Second-degree burns on my neck, back and arms.
- Partial paralysis of my vocal chords.
- Multiple cuts and abrasions.
- Temporary paralysis on my left side.
- Nerve damage.

I am humbled to say, I truly believe the Lord placed within my family, the most precious person to walk His green earth. I am referring to His faithful servant, my Aunt Linda Turbyfill. She and I have always been close, but she stayed faithfully by my side, never leaving the hospital the entire time I was there. She also drove me to therapy before I was able, and traveled with me to San Francisco, California, for my second spinal surgery. Love and devotion like that must be acknowledged! (See Proverbs 27:2)

I didn't understand everything I was going through as I was going through it, but the Lord showed me bits and pieces of His will along the way. The previously stated passage was a great starting point. It showed me how I would be able to react to it all. I would like to go back and revisit the last passage discussed and let's add verse 10. There are several key elements at play in this portion of Scripture. *"And he said unto me, My grace is sufficient for thee: for my strength is made perfect in weakness. Most gladly therefore will I rather glory in my infirmities, that the power of Christ may rest upon me. Therefore I take pleasure in infirmities, in reproaches, in necessities, in persecutions, in distresses for Christ's sake: for when I am weak, then am I strong."*

My first attempt at communication post-crash. It says, "I want a Chevy."

"My grace is sufficient for thee." Wow! What a loaded statement! God's grace was, and always will be, present in my trials. It's often been said that grace is God

giving us what we don't deserve. I know that there is nothing special about me, and God doesn't owe me anything, but in His goodness He promised me, *"I will never leave thee, nor forsake thee,"* (Hebrews 13:5). Even while I was at death's door, God was with me. Psalm 23:4 states, *"Yea, though I walk through the valley of the shadow of death, I will fear no evil: for thou art with me; thy rod and thy staff they comfort me."* With that kind of support, it does give you a little extra strength to push ahead for one more day.

"My strength is made perfect in weakness." Notice, this is **His** strength, not mine. When we are at our weakest moments, God is at His strongest. We are forced to place full reliance on Him and not ourselves. It's something that can't be fully explained; rather it has to be experienced. When **you** are at the end of **your** abilities, strength, hope, etc… that's when **God** can step in and flex **His** muscles. It's the very nature of God to show His creation how great He is. Read Psalm 86:5: *"For thou, Lord, art good, and ready to forgive; and plenteous in mercy unto all them that call upon thee."* God is good and "standing at the ready," waiting to show Himself to each and every one of us. What a blessing! **His** strength is how I would make it.

The *how* I should react was the tougher pill to swallow. It's not easy to smile when going through a fiery trial. Nonetheless, the passage emphasized says, *"Most gladly therefore will I rather glory in my infirmities [the how], that the power of Christ may rest upon me [the why]."* If I can joyfully accept the hard times that have come my way, I am promised a special vantage point from which I can watch the power of Christ work in my life! It, too, is something that cannot be fully explained; rather, it has to be experienced. I will admit, prior to March 13, 2012, I wouldn't have asked for any of this. Since then, however, I have had the pleasure of seeing the Lord work in me and through me in ways I would have never imagined.

This book was entitled *Trial by Fire* for a reason. I was pulled from a burning car just mere seconds before it was fully engulfed, receiving some burns in the process. My trial the Lord chose for me to go through was both a literal and spiritual fire. In helping me endure the sometimes painful process (physical, mental, and emotional), the Lord began showing me truths in His word, and it seemed as though they came when I needed them most. Not only did He promise me that He would see me through it (Hebrews 13:5), He also declared in I Corinthians 10:13, *"...but God is faithful, who will not suffer you to be tempted above that ye are able; but will with the temptation also make a way to escape, that ye may be able to bear it."*

The Bible has a lot to say about fiery trials. For now, the Lord wanted me to look at *my* understanding of why it happened. It is in our human nature to ask *why* when going through a hardship. God understands this about us and anticipates such fears and uncertainties. I Peter 4:12-13 helped me accept my fate and settle the *why* in my heart and mind more than any other passage of Scripture: *"Beloved, think it not strange concerning the fiery trial which is to try you, as though some strange thing happened unto you: But rejoice, inasmuch as ye are partakers of Christ's sufferings; that, when his glory shall be revealed, ye may be glad also with exceeding joy."*

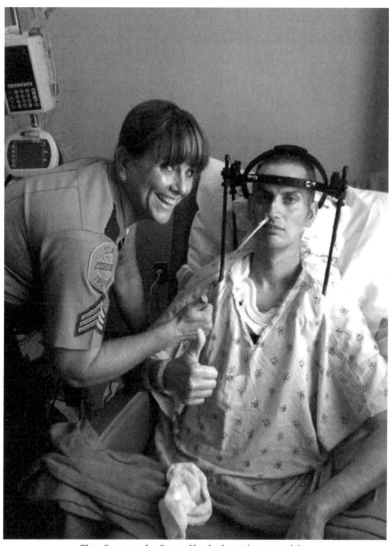

Then Sgt., now Lt. Stacey Heatherly paying me a visit.

There is so much at work in this passage! First, he calls me His beloved. One thing this job has taught me is that there isn't much love in this world and it is definitely lacking for those who stand in the thin blue line. But HE loves me and that's all that matters. He also gives some hefty advice. God says twice in the passage that fiery trials aren't by chance. The old saying referenced in the introduction is, "Did it ever occur to you that nothing occurs to God?" God allowed me to almost be killed and go through a painful rehab process for a reason. It wasn't by accident that the accident happened – it was by divine providence. It was time to sit back and watch the glory of the Lord be revealed as He gave me joy in my troubles!

This brought me to the next stage in God revealing His will to me. Perhaps the greatest, yet simplest *why* was answered when I read Philippians 1:12: *"But I would ye should understand, brethren, that the things which happened unto me have fallen out rather unto the furtherance of the gospel."* Had I not gone through this, I would not have had the opportunity to share the Gospel of the Lord like I have today. My ultimate goals for you, the reader, are to understand your eternal options and fully comprehend what it means to be saved. The Lord saw fit to let me experience what I underwent as a means to share His good news with all who would read this book. His ways are not our ways for sure, but they are better!

Speaking of fiery trials, the Lord does say a lot about the refiner's fire. The refiner's fire works to burn away impurities in order to produce a more pure product. Consider with me what the Scriptures have to say about it. Isaiah 48:10 says, *"Behold, **I have refined thee**, but not with silver; **I** have chosen thee **in** the furnace of affliction."* It's a holy thing to read this passage and realize that God picked me out, that *He* did the refining and that *He* was there with me (notice it says *He* chose me *in* the furnace of affliction).

Affliction is never pleasant. Yet in the hands of the perfect Master, it works a perfect work, better than one could ever imagine. It kind of reminds me of that "His ways are not our ways" thing again! For a good Bible study on the nature of God as a purifier of men, study the following passages. Zechariah 13:9: *"And I will bring the third part through the fire, and will refine them as silver is refined, and will try them as gold is tried: they shall call on my name, and I will hear them: I will say, It is my people: and they shall say, The LORD is my God."* Malachi 3:2-3 says, *"But who may abide the day of his coming? and who shall stand when he appeareth? for he is like a refiner's fire, and like fulllers' soap: And he shall sit as a refiner and purifier of silver: and he shall purify the sons of Levi, and purge them as gold and silver, that they may offer unto the LORD an offering in righteousness."*

Perhaps the greatest blessing of all was seeing what He promised would be the end result of enduring the fiery trial. Job 23:10 and 14 deliver this message: *"But he knoweth the way that I take: when he hath tried me, I shall come forth as gold. ... For he performeth the thing that is appointed for me: and many such things are with him."* I am promised to become a better person when I come through the fire than before entering *if* (that's a big if!) I submit my will to Him.

Possibly the most beautiful thing the Lord showed me from His word is the truth and reality about His unfailing presence with me *in* my trial. Just as He was *in* the fiery furnace with Shadrach, Meshach, and Abednego in the book of Daniel, the Lord was with me and orchestrated EVERYTHING that happened *in* my rescue. Not only did He have the paramedics immediately on scene, the KPD officers shortly to follow, Mr. Stevens with his box cutter to cut my seatbelt and Mr. Lewis to assist, but take a moment and look at the cover photo – did you notice my driver's door standing wide open? The impact of the semi crushed the entire cruiser in an accordion effect. No other door would open. For all intents and purposes, my door shouldn't have been able to be opened. If my door had jammed up like all the other doors I would not be here today. All the concerned citizens, police, fire and EMT personnel wouldn't have been able to save my life. That door opening was THE key. God showed me this in Revelation 3:7-8: *"And to the angel of the church in Philadelphia write; These things saith he* [Jesus] *that is holy, he that is true, **he that hath the key** of David, **he that openeth, and no man shutteth; and shutteth, and no man openeth**; I know thy works: **behold, I have set before thee an open door, and no man can shut it**: for thou hast a little strength, and hast kept my word, and hast not denied my name."*

Humanly speaking, two men opened the door of my cruiser that morning when they extricated me from the vehicle, but it was *only* possible because GOD allowed that door to open! Personally, the true depth of this passage has not sunk in, and I don't think during this lifetime I will ever attain the knowledge to discern just how powerful it really is! It was as if God said to me, "I know you, Lowell, you are one of mine. I know your works, your desire to aid your fellow man. You have been faithful to me and have not denied me. Right now, you have no strength. Behold, I set before you an open door that no man can open or shut. Here, now, for you my son, are some of my servants, and they will help you." God provided *An Open Door*...that to this day will not shut!

Behold the door that no man can close! (Notice the bungee cord.)

In closing, a friend shared an old hymn with me that I felt was fitting to put here. Just like the word of God is timeless, an old hymn can also be that way. This particular song was written in 1787, yet it spoke to my heart as if it had been written in 2012! Please enjoy!

HOW FIRM A FOUNDATION

How firm a foundation, ye saints of the Lord,
Is laid for your faith in His excellent word!
What more can He say than to you He hath said,
To you who for refuge to Jesus have fled?

In every condition, in sickness, in health,
And poverty's vale, or abounding in wealth,
At home and abroad, on the land, on the sea,
As thy days may demand, shall thy strength ever be.

Fear not, I am with thee; O, be not dismayed;
For I am thy God, and will still give thee aid;
I'll strengthen thee, help thee, and cause thee to stand,
Upheld by My righteous, omnipotent hand.

When through the deep waters, I call thee to go,
The rivers of sorrow shall not overflow;
*For **I will be with thee, thy trials to bless,***
And sanctify to thee thy deepest distress.

When through fiery trials, thy pathway shall lie,
My grace, all-sufficient, shall be thy supply;
The flame shall not hurt thee; I only design,
Thy dross to consume, and thy gold to refine.

The soul that on Jesus doth lean for repose,
I will not, I will not, desert to his foes;
That soul, though all hell should endeavor to shake,
I'll never, no never, no never forsake.

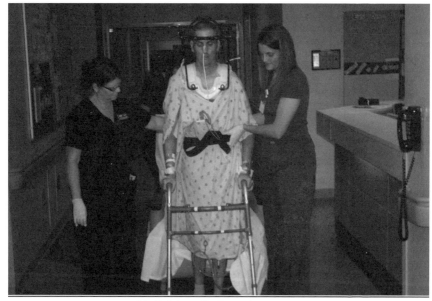

My first steps after the crash.

Rehabilitation and physical therapy, AKA "Learning to live again 101."

Chapter 9

FORGIVENESS

"And forgive us our debts, as we forgive our debtors."
Matthew 6:12

After several days of being either unconscious or semiconscious, the doctors began feeling optimistic enough to change my prognosis from doubtful to probable. At first, they had warned my family that I would probably die, but through God's grace it seemed now, I would make it. Boy, after an event like this, "make it" really seemed quite vague. Since that day it has been a long journey of recovery and therapy. I see a speech therapist weekly to keep my voice muscles strong after having suffered partial paralysis of my vocal chords, an injury that also causes difficulty in swallowing food. I attend physical therapy twice a week, and will need to do so quite possibly for the rest of my life. Also, as this book was being written – this chapter even – I have once again undergone high risk spinal surgery to remove the hardware used to rebuild my neck. The process is supposed to help me regain more mobility but also brings with it even more physical therapy. "Make it;" yep, that means something totally different from this vantage point.

While I may never physically be the same, go on patrol or supervise a shift again, there are several things that are different – even better. As was discussed in the previous chapter, there is a reason for the refiner's fire. It works to purify whatever element is put in the crucible. It burns off the dross and impurities to produce a purer product. The heat will feel unbearable at times, but the end result is priceless!

Consider with me the value God has placed on His own holy word. In Psalm 138:2 the Scripture says, *"...for thou hast magnified thy word above all thy name."* Understanding how high and holy the name of God is, it's a profound thought that God places His *word* above that *name*! Even more profound than that is how God sent His own word through the refiner's fire. Psalm 12:6-7 says this: ***"The words of the LORD are** pure words: as silver **tried in a furnace** of earth, purified seven times. Thou shalt keep them, O LORD, thou shalt preserve them from this generation for ever."* Evil men have tried for thousands of years to stamp out the word of God, yet it is the number one book to ever be produced.

The thought hit me, if a holy God who esteems His word above His own name was willing to put that very word through a furnace, why shouldn't I be willing to be purified? God truly does know better than I and He knew that I needed to be purged. That didn't make the trial any easier per se, but it did help me to put things into perspective and come to grips with my new reality. I love the badge, I love the job, but I wouldn't be doing it anymore. To a certain degree it's even a life risk to get out and drive on a daily basis. Yet NONE of that means that I have to give up on life and stop living! God doesn't take away one thing without giving us something better.

Now, I know what just about any LEO with half a brain is thinking at the moment: How could anything be better than this job? To a point I agree. Consider the essence of being an officer of the law. We are public servants, and it is our duty to serve the public in whatever capacity possible. I know we may not be "bobbies" but the nine principles of community policing developed by Sir Robert Peel and embraced by modern law enforcement agencies are at the essence of this idea. To the degree we involve the general public in our duties, we aid them in any way we can.

Since the accident the Lord has sent many new relationships into my life. Through the telling of my story I have been able to help and inspire more people than I ever imagined. Frankie's death brought to me the opportunity to influence and mentor many young people. While it may not be in the way I trained vigorously and worked for nearly twenty years, my opportunities for public service still continue. It has definitely taken some getting used to and, humanly speaking, it still can be difficult to deal with the adjustments. Nevertheless, I know I am in God's hands, doing His work, and am happy to do it however He sees fit.

While all of this may sound nice and flowery, the facts remain unchanged. My first opportunity to help someone after the wreck was my first big test to see whether the refiner's fire had any effect or not. I'm speaking about Mr. Eric Lewis, the driver of the truck that struck me that night. He wasn't intoxicated or under the influence of any drugs, he simply made the mistake of falling asleep at the wheel. That was all – nothing more, nothing less. He had no malicious intent, he wasn't trying to hurt or kill me; it was an accident, pure and simple. Mr. Lewis is one of the many that helped to save my life in those wee hours of that fateful morning. If not for his actions, I might not be here to tell this story. Yes, the human element comes in to play sometimes and I struggle with how dramatically different my life is, but we all make mistakes and need FORGIVENESS.

In a way, when forgiving Mr. Lewis I was also helping myself. There is an unexplainable peace inside when you are able to let something go instead of allowing it to gnaw at you. In August, just one year and five months after the crash, I was able to write a victim impact statement to be presented before the court by Assistant District Attorney General Leland Price on behalf of Mr. Lewis. This is what it said:

"I have no animosity or hard feelings toward Mr. Lewis and I do not believe that incarcerating him would accomplish anything. Therefore, I have no objection to him being granted probation.

I have no doubt that he regrets the collision that injured me and wished it had never happened. I would like to think that Mr. Lewis did not mean to drive while he was impaired from being tired and sleepy. I would like to think that he simply used poor judgment like so many other people I have seen during my years with the Highway Patrol who have injured or killed themselves and others simply by not taking the time to drive responsibly and carefully. It is very important that people exercise the privilege of driving only when they are up to the task, which means being well rested, free from distractions like texting, talking on the phone or doing anything else that impairs them in anyway. To do otherwise is being reckless and dangerous. If drivers are tired and sleepy they should stop and rest. To those drivers who drink and do drugs, stay home. There is no reason to be on the road driving. You could save a life simply by stopping, resting or staying home.

Mr. Lewis,

I have not asked the court to impose any type of community service on you, but I would strongly encourage you to volunteer your time to help disabled veterans, veteran's groups and other charities or volunteer groups wherever you may have an interest. During my convalescence since being injured, I have found great personal satisfaction and joy from helping veterans, their families and other charitable organizations. Of course, what you do is up to you.

Mr. Lewis, I forgive you and hope that you will use the rest of your life being productive and live the kind of life that would make your parents proud and that pleases God.

With best wishes,

Lowell Russell"

I'm the type of person that likes things to run peacefully in life. I could have held a grudge against Mr. Lewis but that wouldn't have done me any good. Bitterness would have just caused me to age quicker, and in this condition I sure didn't need that! Every day when I wake up (Thank you, Lord!) and go outside I'm reminded of the wreck by not seeing my THP patrol car sitting in the driveway where it had been parked for nearly 15 years. For a while after the crash I was quite torn up (no pun intended) that I wasn't putting on the uniform, hopping into my patrol car and heading to work. Instead, I put on a t-shirt, blue jeans, and hopped into my trusty ol' pickup truck to go to therapy in order to help me slowly regain strength and endurance to recover to the best of my abilities. On February 28, 2014, I had the aforementioned second neck surgery and had to start back at the bottom of the rehabilitation chain. The need for frequent rehab is a daily reminder that life has now changed – dramatically! But, as my good friend and co-author of this book says, "When true forgiveness is present, bitterness is absent."

When looking at the scriptural teachings on forgiveness the Lord brings some eternal truths to light. Forgiveness is a subject God wants us to learn; it's a big deal to Him. Forgiveness is mentioned over a hundred times in Scripture! If our heavenly Father is repeating Himself that much, maybe we should pay attention!

The Lord pointed out to me four concepts about forgiveness. First, as peace officers we love Matthew 5:9: *"Blessed are the peacemakers: for they shall be called the children of God."* If we are honest students of the Bible, we must read on to the next chapter. Matthew 6:12 says, *"And forgive us our debts, as we forgive our debtors."* A reason forgiveness is so important to God is that it cuts to the root of man's two greatest weaknesses: Pride and Hypocrisy. It deals with pride because there are times we need to be forgiven when we have wronged someone; I know I have. If we are all truthful, we will admit WE ALL have wronged someone along the way. Hypocrisy is exposed by revealing a lack of forgiveness toward someone while expecting it towards ourselves. For more information on this read Matthew 18:23-35; it will truly put some things into perspective.

The second thing about forgiveness is how it speaks to the very nature of Christ. When He was dying on the cross as the payment for our sins He cried out, *"...Father, forgive them; for they know not what they do..."* (Luke 23:34). Even in the throes of death, forgiveness was on the mind of God. Psalm 86:5 teaches us this: *"For thou, Lord, art good, and ready to forgive; and plenteous in mercy unto all them that call upon thee."* Quite often we forgive, but it's like pulling teeth to get us to because we aren't ready. If we are to be more Christ-like in our lives we need to be ready to forgive and give mercy to those in need of it. You will appreciate and truly be thankful when you are on the receiving end of forgiveness once you have learned to quickly and joyfully apply it from the giving end.

The third principle of Christ-like forgiveness takes an extra step into the "advanced class" when we see *how* we are to forgive. Ephesians 4:32 says, *"And be ye kind one to another, tenderhearted, forgiving one another, even as God for Christ's sake hath forgiven you."* I am to forgive as Christ forgave. He forgave the sins of the whole world. Why then, should I have such a difficult time forgiving one trespass against me? May God help us to practice this important essence of forgiveness in our personal lives.

A dear friend showed me a passage on forgiveness just a few weeks before my second neck surgery. It was as if the Lord said to me, "Lowell, this is what you did for Eric Lewis." II Corinthians 2:7 says, *"So that contrariwise ye ought rather to forgive him, and comfort him, lest perhaps such a one should be swallowed up with overmuch sorrow."* This is the fourth concept. It was important from the very mind of God that I forgive Mr. Lewis *and* comfort him through that forgiveness to prevent him from being overtaken in guilt and grief for his simple mistake, and so he could have the opportunity to move on with his life.

From all that I know of him, Mr. Lewis is a good man and there will always be an element of sorrow in his heart. I don't need to add to that by having bitterness and hatred in my heart towards him. By forgiving him, I did what little human part I can to ease any pain he may carry. I cannot, however, take any glory for it; it must all go to God.

Through this book, my objective is for my story to be a help to my brothers and sisters of the thin blue line. In addition, I want to encourage any other first responders, military personnel, or civilians reading this book. Do know that no matter how dark the path is for you to trod, no matter how deep the valley, no matter how depressing the situation, *Forgiveness* is possible through God.

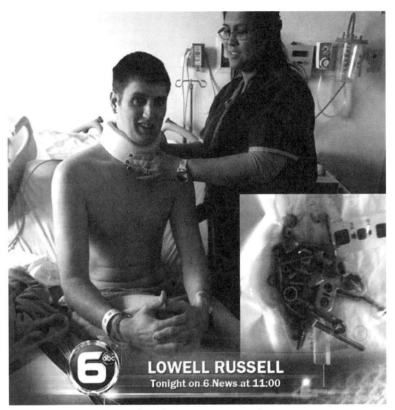

Second surgery was a success!

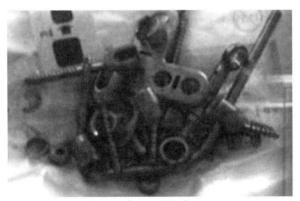

Close-up of my neck hardware.

Chapter 10

PEACE AND THANKSGIVING

"And the very God of peace sanctify you wholly…"
I Thessalonians 5:23

When pondering about the subject matter of this chapter I had a host of emotions surface in my heart. While I must admit that this book has had quite a few dark and sad moments, they each served a purpose. The intent is not to make one feel sorrow or pity for me, but to show just how big God really is and how He can bring you through anything you may face in life. Both personally and professionally, I feel I have faced more death than I care to truly contemplate. The deaths that hurt the most, however, are the ones that hit the closest to home – family.

Peace – what does it mean? While I'm not going to try to give a detailed philosophical, theological, or dictionary definition, I do feel that my personal experiences and spiritual beliefs have afforded me the ability to speak somewhat on the matter. If I were to try and simply define peace, it would be this: Going through any level of stress and being able to initially react as any normal human being would, whether that be anxiety, fear, anger, sorrow, etc…; being able to regroup and refocus; finding contentment with whatever lot you find yourself in; moving forward and maintaining a positive outlook.

While what I just stated sounds really good, I truly understand that those words are much easier spoken than lived. An old preacher once said, "Your walk talks and your talk talks, but your walk talks louder than your talk talks!" I have learned by experience that it is sometimes easier to talk about peace than it is to actually live in it. I didn't choose to be born into poverty. I didn't decide to have learning struggles growing up. I didn't ask for my parents to divorce. I would rather my mother, father, and Frankie were still with me today. I wish my health and physical condition were what they once were. However, experience has taught me that I don't have to live in the world of "wishful thinking." I can (through God's grace, mercy, and peace) live just as normal, healthy (mental), and fulfilling a life as if I had never gone through anything difficult.

God's word has much to say about peace. He mentions it over four hundred times in Scripture! This is a topic near and dear to the heart of our Creator, for a great reason. He said that everyone, good and evil, will have to endure hard times. It's an essential spiritual fact to the human experience; again, things don't happen to us by coincidence. For an excellent study on this concept, cross reference Matthew 5:45 with a review of Ecclesiastes 3. Knowing that God is in control and He is doing a work far greater than our finite minds are able to comprehend is a settling reality if you have the faith to accept it. Understanding and accepting this fact is the first step to being able to gain peace with your situation.

Consider with me a few select passages from the Scriptures about peace. While this first one doesn't say "peace" per se, it screams its definition. Philippians 4:11 says, *"Not that I speak in respect of want: for I have learned,* [experience] *in whatsoever state I am, therewith to be content."* There was a great reason why the Apostle Paul could say this. After being imprisoned, beaten, shipwrecked, left for dead, snake bit, and many other trials, he learned (by experience) that God was in control, working His own work that was far greater than anything he personally could produce. When we learn to "let go and let God" in our lives, peace is the natural byproduct.

A blessed thought is that, while God may send trials into our lives for various reasons, He does desire for us to have peace in the midst of those trials. I Corinthians 14:33 states, *"For God is not the author of confusion, but of peace, as in all churches of the saints."* Contrast that with II Thessalonians 3:16: *"Now the Lord of peace himself give you peace always by all means. The Lord be with you all."* God loves us, and while we must endure hardships during our lives, it isn't His will for us to stay discouraged, confused, hurt, angry, etc... It's His will for us to stay focused on Him for strength and victory. Isaiah 26:3 says, *"Thou wilt keep him in perfect peace, whose mind is stayed on thee: because he trusteth in thee."* What a blessed thought to know the Lord desires peace in our lives despite turmoil.

Quite possibly the most incredible passage on peace is found in Philippians 4:7 and 9: *"And the peace of God, which passeth all understanding, shall keep your hearts and minds through Christ Jesus... and the God of peace shall be with you."* When you find true, lasting peace you will discover that it is something unexplainable. It is a special grace that comes only from the living God. Peace is not something that you as a person can manufacture. It's not something that a friend or family member can give you. It's not something you can find in a self-help book. God gives His peace because He *is* the God of peace. Once you've discovered it, you'll know it. It may be unexplainable, but it is attainable. True peace lies solely *in* God.

If you have noticed, there is a word that has come in to play over and over again in the last few pages: Experience. Experience teaches, strengthens, and prepares us for each new step in life. Experiences like those that the Lord has allowed me to go through have molded me into the person the Lord wants me to be today. On the outside I am a beat up, worn down person compared to who I was a few years ago. Inside, I am stronger than ever. I have the peace of God dwelling in me.

When building a building, you must have the proper tools, right? Think about it for a second; just how far do you think you're going to get using a flathead screwdriver to put sixteen penny nails into a two-by-four or by using a nail gun as a level? Follow the train of thought with me: God gives us trials as part of His will. God desires us to have His peace in our trials. So, how do we do it? How do we get this unexplainable peace? The tool you need is thankfulness.

It sounds like you may have the wrong tool in hand, doesn't it? Perhaps, maybe we switched conversations? I assure you we didn't. As unusual as it may seem, peace and thanksgiving go hand in hand. The Bible even shows them "hanging out" together in the same passage. Colossians 3:15 says, *"And let the peace of God rule in your hearts, to the which also ye are called in one body; and be ye thankful."* The peace of God can have free reign in our lives when we live thankful lives.

Now, here's where the rubber really meets the road. Life sure is easy when you're "up on the mountain." You can see for miles and you may feel like you've got things all figured out. At times like this we are thankful creatures. "Thank you, God, for my family. Thank you for my job. Thank you for my health." These are the prayers we like to pray. But, wait… what about the moments when we are "down in the valley?" Absent is the prayer that goes something like this: "Dear Lord, I want to thank you for all you have given me and done for me. I want to thank you for taking my loved ones from me in death. I want to thank you for letting me lose my job. Thank you, Lord, for the cancer you have given me."

Why are we so quick to thank the Lord for the good but not the bad? Job wisely said, *"…What? shall we receive good at the hand of God, and shall we not receive evil?… Though he slay me, yet will I trust in him…"* (Job 2:10; 13:15). Here's how thankfulness works with peace: I can't tell you how it works, it just does! Remember Philippians 4:7, *"…the peace of God, which passeth all understanding?"* THAT'S IT! When you can thank God for the bad stuff, a calm and settling presence will come over you that you cannot explain.

If you want further proof that this is how it works, let me leave you with an appropriate philosophical passage from the Bible. I Thessalonians 5:18 says, *"**In every thing give thanks**: for this is the will of God in Christ Jesus concerning you."* As much as it is the will of God for you to suffer, it is the will of God that you have peace in your trial. As much as it is the will of God for you to have peace in your trial, it is His will that you thank Him for the trial. In turn, He promises you what the world craves but cannot find – peace. *Peace and Thanksgiving*; it's real, you have to EXPERIENCE it!

The Bible lists in Romans chapter one, those who are unthankful with those who distort the image of God. As this book draws to a close, I would feel remiss if I didn't take a moment to say, "Thank you," not only to the many heroes who saved my life on the road that night, but also to the many doctors, medical professionals, and therapists at the University of Tennessee Hospital, Patricia Neal Rehabilitation Center, St. Francis Memorial Hospital (San Francisco, California), and the many various rehab clinics I've frequented. Many thanks to them for all they have done, to not only save my life, but also to make it as pain free and mobile as possible. Without their love, devotion, and sacrifice I wouldn't be able to do what I do today. My life would not be possible without the passion you have for your respective professions. Thank you!

I had one last blessing to share as a point of encouragement to all our LEOs, first responders, and military personnel. It gets tough, but hang in there. God has a special work He is doing *in you and through you*. Recently, I heard an old southern gospel song and found the lyrics very fitting to aid in bringing my story to its conclusion:

KEEP ON THE FIRING LINE

*Oh, you **must fight, be brave** against all evil,*
Never run, nor even lag behind;
If you would win for God and the right,
Just keep on the firing line.

Chaplain Grady and I just prior to my second neck surgery.

Appendix
About the LCpl Frankie Watson Memorial Scholarship Fund

Frankie Watson gave the ultimate sacrifice for the freedom of this great nation on September 24, 2011. To honor this brave warrior, for all that he gave, a memorial scholarship fund has been put into place in his memory.

Each year a student from Sequoyah High School in Monroe County, TN, (where Frankie graduated) who chooses to attend college in order to train for a career in public service, is selected to be awarded a scholarship to help pay towards their expenses.

Proceeds from the sale of this book are applied to this fund. If you would like to donate or sponsor a student, please write to the address listed below, or mail a check or money order to:

Frankie Watson Memorial Scholarship Fund
PO Box 777
Vonore, TN 37885

About the Cover

Jerry Traxler has a special talent for being able to express the vision of the authors. If you would like to contact him regarding a future project you can email him at: jerry@trueblue.net.

Lance Corporal and Officer Franklin "Frankie" Namon Watson.

Appendix

Glossary of terms

For those of you who may be reading this book but do not have a law enforcement or military background, we have added this glossary of terms section, to familiarize you with some common "cop lingo" that is found throughout this book. Thanks, and enjoy!

Military time – Please refer to the below listed chart.

Military Time	Standard Time
0000	12:00 AM
0100	01:00 AM
0200	02:00 AM
0300	03:00 AM
0400	04:00 AM
0500	05:00 AM
0600	06:00 AM
0700	07:00 AM
0800	08:00 AM
0900	09:00 AM
1000	10:00 AM
1100	11:00 AM
1200	12:00 PM
1300	01:00 PM
1400	02:00 PM
1500	03:00 PM
1600	04:00 PM
1700	05:00 PM
1800	06:00 PM

1900	07:00 PM
2000	08:00 PM
2100	09:00 PM
2200	10:00 PM
2300	11:00 PM

Bobbies – Nickname given to British Police Officers, derived from the father of modern policing, Sir Robert Peel.

BOLO – "Be one the Lookout" This is an alert sent to law enforcement agencies from another agency to be watching for a missing, person, suspect, vehicle, etc... whenever a crime or critical incident occurs.

Field Training – Once academy is completed, an officer must endure a rigorous testing phase in real life patrol to determine if he/she is ready to commit to life on patrol in an effective and safe manor, and has the competence and confidence required to perform the job effectively. Field training usually last for several months.

FTO – Field Training Officer; also commonly used to refer to the field training program an officer goes through post-academy.

KFD – Knoxville Fire Department

KPD – Knoxville Police Department

LEO – Law Enforcement Officer

MVA – Motor Vehicle Accident

On Scene – This identifies that an officer has reached the destination of the call to which he was dispatched.

OPR – Office of Professional Responsibility, AKA Office of professional Standards, AKA Internal Affairs. When a complaint, whether personal, professional or criminal, is filed against an officer, the OPR is responsible for internally investigating the claim to determine whether it is valid or invalid, and if there is any disciplinary or actions or criminal charges necessary the officer.

Probation – When a criminal offender is released from detention, he/she may be required to register with a probation officer with whom they will be under supervision concerning the conditions of their behavior, in order to avoid further jail time.

Ride Along – Most agencies have a "ride along" program that allows citizens without a criminal record or criminal affiliation to ride with a patrol officer to experience the uniqueness of the job or to determine if it is a career that they would like to join.

THP – Tennessee Highway Patrol

Appendix

Tennessee Highway Patrol Ten Codes

10-1 Receiving Poorly
10-2 Receiving Well
10-3 Stop Transmitting
10-4 Acknowledgement
10-5 Relay
10-6 Busy
10-7 Out of Service
10-8 In Service
10-9 Repeat
10-10 Out of Unit
10-11 Dispatching to Rapidly
10-12 Officials or Visitors Present
10-13 Advise Weather Conditions
10-14 Convoy or Escort
10-15 Prisoner in Custody
10-16 Transporting Subject
10-17 Advise Road Conditions
10-18 Complete Present Assignment as Quickly as Possible
10-19 Advise Traffic Conditions
10-20 Location
10-21 Call Station R (Residence)
10-22 Meal/Break
10-23 Nature Call
10-24 Felony Criminal Interdiction
10-25 Do You Have Contact With _____?
10-26 Check Driver License History
10-27 Check Driver License Status
10-28 Check Vehicle Registration
10-29 Check for Stolen or Wanted

10-30 Does Not Conform to Rules or Regulations

10-31 Hit on 10-29. Is it Safe to Copy Information?

10-32 Breathalyzer

10-33 Emergency Traffic-Clear Radio Net

10-34 Officer in Trouble, Location

_____

10-35 Confidential Information

10-36 Correct Time

10-37 Operator on Duty

10-38 Request Backup (Not 10-34)

10-39 Theft of Property

10-40 Vandalism

10-41 Lewd/Indecent Activity

10-42 Assist(ing) Other Unity/Agency

10-43 Want Officer – Investigation

10-44 Stolen Vehicle

10-45 Property Damage Vehicle Crash

10-46 Personal Injury Vehicle Crash

10-47 Ambulance

10-48 Wrecker

10-49 Driving Under the Influence (DUI)

10-50 No Traffic Here

10-51 Positive Response on Criminal History (Not 10-31)

10-52 Armed Robbery

10-53 Hit and Run

10-54 Citizen Complaint of _____ (Specify)

10-55 Kidnapping

10-56 Rape

10-57 Reckless/Unsafe Operation of a Vehicle

10-58 Drunk

10-59 Lunacy

10-60 Missing Person
10-61 Suspicious Person
10-62 Special Assignment (Specify Assignment or Authority)
10-63 Grant Overtime (Specify Type and Location)
10-64 Radio Net Clear
10-65 Fight in Progress
10-66 Administrative/Supervisory Duties
10-67 Court Duty
10-68 Training
10-69 Domestic Disturbance
10-70 Dead on Arrival (DOA)
10-71 Vehicular Homicide
10-72 Suicide
10-73 Checkpoint
10-74 Blood Run

10-75 Commercial Vehicle Inspection
10-76 Do You Have Traffic for ____?
10-77 Radio Repairs at ____
10-78 Car Repairs/Service at ____
10-79 Car Wash at ____
10-80 Stationary Observation at ____
10-81 Stopping Violator
10-82 Stopping Suspicious Vehicle
10-83 Assist(ing) Motorist/Citizen
10-84 Medical Call/Situation
10-85 Serve(ing) Warrant
10-86 Abandon Vehicle
10-87 Improperly Parked Vehicle

10-88 Obstructing Roadway/Object in Road
10-89 Disabled Vehicle
10-90 Fire Apparatus
10-91 Fire (Vehicle, Structure, etc.)
10-92 Rescue Unit
10-93 Crash Investigation Follow-up
10-94 Felony Investigation
10-95 Misdemeanor Investigation
10-96 Other Type Investigation
10-97 Arrived at Scene
10-98 Finished with Last Assignment
10-99 Pursuit

Appendix

Website Links

http://www.knoxnews.com/news/local-news/thp-troopers-rescue-from-fiery-i-40-crash-was-of

http://www.msnewsnow.com/story/17148669/trooper-hurt-in-knoxville-highway-crash

http://www.thedailytimes/com/news/trooper-sgt-lowell-russell-recovering-from-injuries-in-i-/article_84459903-c79a-5e5f-9439-7bc6ef09851c.html

http://www.local8now.com/home/headlines/Bucky_Covingt on_to_play_benefit_show_for_Sgt_Lowell_Russell_145927 845.html

http://theknoxvillejournal.com/sgt-lowell-russell-makes-first-personal-appearances-after-crash/

http://www.wate.com/story/17143583/driver-facing-charges-after-fiery-wreck-injured-trooper-on-i-40

http://archive.wbir.com/rss/article/285069/2/Injured-THP-trooper-forgives-driver-who-hit-him-supports-probation

http://www.knoxnews.com/news/thp-sgt-lowell-russell-continues-therapy

http://www.policeone.com/Officer-Safety/articles/6176146-A-year-after-near-fatal-accident-trooper-works-to-get-life-back/

http://www.wbir.com/story/news/local/2014/03/08/lowell-russell-spinal-surgery-home/6220307/

http://www.local8now.com/home/headlines/Sgt-Lowell-Russell-2-years-later-250234471.html

http://www.wbir.com/story/news/local/2014/03/13/lowell-russell-crash-two-years/6388569/

http://www.advocateanddemocrat.com/news/article_62df1f6e-5f2d-5a9d-9403-e55d58ed68df.html

https://news.tn.gov/node/6644

http://www.advocateanddemocrat.com/news/article_738f4285-f4dd-5e43-8864-426870e0b25b.html

http://www.advocateanddemocrat.com/news/article_89d1adcc-c4c9-5c2b-8472-d566f538b1f8.html

http://www.wate.com/story/19322953/knox-family-drops-lawsuit-against-thp-trooper-in-sons-death

http://www.wfmynews2.com/story/news/nation/2014/05/13/move-over-law-message/9065213/

http://www.chestercountyindependent.com/find-the-good-and-praise-it-frankie-watson-and-lowell-russell-cms-17794

http://www.policeone.com/police-heroes/articles/5938691-Tenn-cops-pull-trooper-from-burning-car-honored/

http://www.policeone.com/Officer-Safety/articles/5321870-911-tape-Responders-battled-clock-to-save-trooper/

http://media.knoxnews.com/media/static/0321_911call_troop
er.mp3

http://www.jems.com/article/news/paramedics-honored-aid-
trooper-after-cra

http://www.knoxnews.com/news/local-news/gov-bill-
haslam-visits-critically-injured-state

http://www.knoxnews.com/news/local-news/thp-honors-
those-who-came-to-troopers-aid

http://www.local8now.com/home/headlines/Florida-trucker-
indicted-in-Lowell-Russell-crash-
193869041.html?mobile=yes&device=ipad

http://www.wftv.com/news/news/local/orlando-trucker-
indicted-crash-severely-injured-tn/nWcb8/

http://www.heraldtribune.com/article/20130228/APN/13022
80728

http://www.sfgate.com/news/crime/article/Fla-trucker-
indicted-in-severe-injury-crash-4316044.php

http://www.wate.com/story/21425248/truck-driver-indicted-
in-accident-that-seriously-injured-trooper-lowell-russell

http://www.wbir.com/news/article/256893/2/Trucker-
indicted-in-fiery-crash-that-injured-trooper

http://www.wcyb.com/news/Florida-truck-driver-indicted-
for-2012-crash-into-trooper/-/14590844/19119844/-
/qho762z/-/index.html

http://www.knoxnews.com/news/2013/feb/27/trucker-indicted-in-fiery-crash-that-nearly-thp/

http://www.miamiherald.com/2013/02/28/3258623/fla-trucker-indicted-in-severe.html

http://www.wate.com/story/21899951/highway-411-in-madisonville-dedicated-in-memory-of-lcpl-frankie-watson

http://www.knoxnews.com/news/local-news/friends-family-show-support-for-injured-trooper

http://www.knoxnews.com/news/local-news/friends-family-show-support-for-injured-trooper

https://www.youtube.com/watch?v=iL4JCkFW6j0&safe=active

https://twitter.com/jennifermeckles/status/202170697538211843

http://www.thedailytimes.com/community/blount-county-memorial-day-program-set-for-saturday/article_512a5a9b-03b7-5f35-aa23-46c27d401b7f.html

http://targetednews.com/nl_disp.php?nl_date_id=308114

http://archive.wbir.com/news/article/210927/2/Injured-trooper-gives-thumbs-up-to-Gov-Haslam-during-hospital-visit?odyssey=tab|topnews|bc|large

http://www.wbir.com/video/1508240511001/1/Injured-trooper-winks-at-Gov-Haslam-during-hospital-visit

Frankie Watson's devotional journal he studied while deployed in Afghanistan.

116

Frankie's tombstone with Joshua 1:9 enscribed.

Sept. 28

Dear lowell,

Sucks I'm not 21 yet I would study for that test to become a trooper like urself. I still want the oreo's sent wen you get this letter also a resse fast break bar king size x2 you can get them at the Shell. We have final Drill tomorrow hope we win then we are badd's lol. Is James excited to come to graduation. Will he be in uniform? Cuz if so Id have to salute him, but as soon as I'm done I'm changing into different attire. Make sure you bring my cell phone and sunglasses when you come down for family day. Tell talen + Thomas I'm going to beat them in Call of Duty !!!

P.S Send the stuff when you get this letter. Dnt forget my phone 1 glasses.

Frank

One of many letters home from Frankie while at Paris Island.

118

STATE OF TENNESSEE
DEPARTMENT OF SAFETY AND HOMELAND SECURITY

312 ROSA L. PARKS AVENUE, 23ᴿᴰ FLOOR
NASHVILLE, TN 37243

BILL HASLAM
GOVERNOR

BILL GIBBONS
COMMISSIONER

August 19, 2013

TO: Knox County Court

FROM: Sgt. Lowell Russell

SUBJECT: Victim Impact Statement

I have no animosity or hard feelings toward Mr. Lewis and I do not believe that incarcerating him would accomplish anything. Therefore, I have no objection to him being granted probation.

I have no doubt that he regrets the collision that injured me and wished it had never happened. I would like to think that Mr. Lewis did not mean to drive while he was impaired from being tired and sleepy. I would like to think that he simply used poor judgment like so many other people I have seen during my years with the Highway Patrol who have injured or killed themselves and others simply by not taking the time to drive responsibly and carefully. It is very important that people exercise the privilege of driving only when they are up to the task, which means being well rested, free from distractions like texting, talking on the phone or doing anything else that impairs them in any way. To do otherwise is being reckless and dangerous. If drivers are tired and sleepy they should stop and rest. To those drivers who drink and do drugs, stay home. There is no reason to be on the road driving. You could save a life simply by stopping, resting or staying home.

Mr. Lewis,

I have not asked the Court to impose any type of community service on you, but I would strongly encourage you to volunteer your time to help disabled veterans, Veteran's groups and other charities or volunteer groups wherever you may have an interest. During my convalescence since being injured, I have found great personal satisfaction and joy from helping Veterans, their families and other charitable organizations. Of course, what you do is up to you.

Mr. Lewis, I forgive you and hope that you will use the rest of your life being productive and live the kind of life that would make your parents proud and that pleases God.

With best wishes,

Sgt. Lowell Russell

Sgt. Lowell Russell

Victim Impact Statement for Mr. Eric Lewis.

119

TENNESSEE HIGHWAY PATROL
Critical Incident Response Team

Reconstructionist's Report

C.I.R.T. Case #	1T1471274	**Date:**	April 24, 2012

C.I.R.T. Member / Reconstructionist: Sergeant William T. Fox

The following represents the opinion of the above identified member of the Tennessee Highway Patrol. The opinion is based on the evidence and information available in this case at the time of this writing as well as the education and experience of the individual.

The following conclusions were drawn after examination of all known physical evidence and review of witness accounts of the event that occurred on Interstate 40 west in Knox County:

1.) Eric D. Lewis was the properly restrained operator of a 2007 International Tractor pulling a flat bed semi trailer traveling west on Interstate 40.

2.) Cleotha Nickles was the unrestrained passenger in the sleeper area of Lewis' vehicle.

3.) Lowell Russel was parked on the right shoulder of I-40 west after completing a traffic stop in his marked Tennessee Highway Patrol unit. His emergency lights were activated.

4.) Lewis drifted onto the right shoulder and collided with Russell's patrol unit. Lewis' left front collided with Russell's right rear.

5.) Russell's vehicle was accelerated forwards and across the west bound lanes of I-40 for approximately 270 feet where it came into contact with the center retaining wall. It then continued west for approximately 66 feet where it came to rest facing east.

6.) Lewis' vehicle veered right after impact and traveled up the ditch line for approximately 865 feet before coming to rest partially on the right west bound shoulder of I-40 facing west.

7.) Lewis stated that he had fallen asleep and didn't wake until he had struck the patrol unit.

8.) Blood was withdrawn from Lewis and sent to the Tennessee Bureau Of Investigation's Lab for testing. Both the Official Alcohol and Toxicology results were negative.

9.) I was able to calculate a minimum speed for Lewis' vehicle by using the distance that Russell's patrol unit was moved by Lewis and the industry standard of a coefficient of friction for sliding metal on asphalt. That speed was 69 miles per hour.

10.) It is my opinion that this crash and the injuries sustained by Russell was the direct result of Lewis' careless and reckless operation of his vehicle and not exercising due care.

Synopsis of the crash report.

120

Military Journal

Name: _____

Basic Training: _____

Location: _____

Graduation Date: _____ Class Rank: _____

Height: _____ Weight: _____ 1st Month Pay: _____

Date	Additional Training	Location

Branch of Military: _____

Recruited by: _____

First Rank: _____

First Assignment: _____

First Supervisor: _____

First MOS: _____

Date	Deployments	Location

Top Scores: _____

Medals Earned: _____

_____

1st Commander-In-Chief _____

Law Enforcement Journal

Name: _____

Agency: _____

Rank: _____ Hire Date: _____

Badge #: _____Academy Graduation Date: _____

First Academy Attended: _____

Height:_____ Weight:_____ Pay/Hour:_____

First Field Supervisor: _____

First Sheriff/Chief/Department Head: _____

First Call to Service: _____

First Traffic Stop: _____

First Arrest: _____

Date	Additional Academies	Location

Date	Schools Attended	Location

Date	Schools Attended	Location

Date	Schools Attended	Location

Notes:_____

_____

_____

_____

_____

_____

_____

_____

_____

_____

_____

_____

_____

_____

_____

_____

_____

_____

_____

Notes (cont...)_____

Notes (cont…)_____

Notes (cont…)_____

Notes (cont…)_____

_____

_____

_____

_____

_____

_____

_____

_____

_____

_____

_____

_____

_____

_____

_____

Notes (cont…)_____

_____

_____

_____

_____

_____

_____

_____

_____

_____

_____

_____

_____

_____

_____

_____

_____

Notes (cont…)_____

Notes (cont...) _____

_____

_____

_____

_____

_____

_____

_____

_____

_____

_____

_____

_____

_____

_____

_____

_____

_____